To my friend Frank Ring

who has always
believed as many as
six impossible things
before breakfast.

Hans Alcardi.
Sept 7, 1967

# THE ABILITIES STORY

ALSO BY *Henry Viscardi, Jr.*

A MAN'S STATURE

GIVE US THE TOOLS

A LAUGHTER IN THE LONELY NIGHT

A LETTER TO JIMMY

THE SCHOOL

# THE ABILITIES STORY

*by Henry Viscardi, Jr.*

*Paul S. Eriksson, Inc., New York*

To Charles A. Dana—a statesman in
shaping the challenge for man's dignity

# PREFACE

Abilities was founded in the early fall of 1952, in a vacant garage, on borrowed capital hardly sufficient to start a newspaper stand. Its work force contained no skilled workers, just four disabled men and women. It was started as an eleemosynary corporation and granted tax exemption which was essential if it was to achieve its purpose. By the end of the first year, that little community that began with four men—among whom we had but one usable leg and five usable arms—had grown to 57 workers, and gross sales by the end of the first fiscal year for the products they made amounted to $191,000. By the end of the second year, the community had grown to 104 workers, and gross sales had climbed to $401,000. Among the 104 were every known category of disability. There were no experienced foremen however, no training supervisors, quality control supervisors, or inspectors. Abilities engaged in electronic manufacturing and was coming through the end of the Korean War. Gross business was climbing. By the end of the third year, the community had grown to 163 men and women and sales of goods produced had climbed to $656,000.

Now, in 1967, this group in Abilities is between

450 and 500 workers, and annual sales will average about $3,500,000 per year.

Taking a total of 14 years, I can establish that from this beginning, with the ideal that disabled people could live and work, these people manufactured goods worth $29,259,000. They received salaries of $15,858,000. They paid taxes of $3,332,000. Abilities expended $12,167,000 on insurance programs, rehabilitation, public education, and programs for the benefit of the disabled community. If these disabled people over these 14 years had remained unemployed, we estimate it would have cost the community or the family who supported them $7,362,000. If we add the value of the goods produced and the salaries paid, the taxes, the amount spent for their benefit, and add in what it would have cost to maintain them as unemployed, the total of new wealth which this group returned to the community is approximately $65,000,000.

The remarkable thing is that they did it as unemployable disabled and in a period when the Korean War was ending and when they had to diversify to new techniques and new customers; and they did it without bringing in at the outset the skilled technicians who would make such an evolution in industry possible.

This book is a story not merely of the triumphs but also of some of the mistakes that were made, some of the heartaches in connection with such a venture. It's the closest thing I can think of to *Alice in Wonderland,* for it is an impossible story. Remember when Alice was talking to the Queen, she laughed and she said, "There's no use trying. You can't believe impossible things." The Queen said, "I daresay you haven't had much practice. Why, when I was your age, I always did it for half an hour a day. Sometimes I believed as many as six impossible things before breakfast."

This, then, is a story, like *Alice in Wonderland,* of six impossible things before breakfast. It is a story of a production center of disabled people who rode the crest of the Korean War needs by building components for a military economy on Long Island and then, as it faced the depression, the recession which occurred after the Korean War in the 1950's, regrouped and reorganized to meet these challenges.

It was the dawn of the computer era, and of predictions that machines were putting people out of business. By 1970, some economic Cassandras insisted, unemployment would be greater than in the great depression—the machines would have at last taken over. Even in the banking field, which is part of our story here, automation was taking over with performances that sound almost impossible. In one of Long Island's biggest banks an automatic device reads nine hundred checks a minute as amounts and account numbers on automatic tape are fed to a computer that adjusts the amounts and account numbers and balances.

As Abilities entered into the banking field, we found some seven hundred bookkeepers in one bank had been replaced by ninety programmers and maintenance men who maintain the computers and the tape indexing machines. As the Korean War ended, and as the technology of business and industry changed, it was openly predicted that the new machines, requiring little cooperation from human beings, would cause unprecedented economic and social disorder. And in the mid-1950's, as war production slackened, these examples of human displacement did occur, and we faced a tragic layoff.

And yet, something exciting was happening around us. The new machines and the wealth that they were creating were opening up great new families of jobs. Changes were coming not only in the military manufacturing field (the predominant economy on Long Island), but were also opening up in other areas. Our challenge was to retain our disabled people and to fit them into this changing technology. We could see that now there were many jobs and the services to feed them: programmers, systems analysts, engineers, technicians to operate and service the new machines and to build them. Salesmen were needed to sell them. As we looked around us, we found that to service the people who were building these new automated machines and those who would sell them, and the new opportunities that would open up in industry, some six thousand new kinds of jobs and careers were created between the time we began in 1952 and 1965.

At the same time, we began to see that in banks and insurance companies, office managers couldn't get enough stenographers; hospitals were desperately seeking nurses; schools were short of teachers; teaching machines were needed; restaurants were hunting for chefs, and garages had a crying need for mechanics. In industry, new types of jobs were opening up steadily, not only in the growing service industries, but in the electronic industry, in data processing, in banking and clerical fields, where we could find an outlet for the talents of our disabled people.

In dramatic contrast to the dire predictions of automation and the cutback from the military economy, especially on Long Island, men who worked with their hands didn't become obsolete after all. Factory workers began working overtime. Their work rate has averaged approximately forty-two hours per week because employers can't get enough of them. And as a result, subcontractors such as Abilities are needed to help turn out the products. In spite of the terrible predictions through which we struggled, there are a million more factory workers today than there were in 1963. Jobs are up, too, for others who were supposed to be hard hit. These include the disabled and the hard core of those discriminated against, the unemployed. And if you worry about teenagers, about sixteen percent more are working today than in 1963.

Automation is giving us the greatest prosperity in our history. It has caused acceleration and, in fact, revolutions in education, in government fiscal policy, in business management, and provided opportunities for those who are disabled and disenfranchised in many ways.

In the face of this changing technology, those of us who are interested in work centers for the disabled had best realize that it's not enough to adhere to the old clichés which indicate that the disabled are good workers, they're on time, and they have less absenteeism. In the face of changing technology, new jobs, and new requirements, this is hardly enough if we are to survive. The fact that we are running a work center for the disabled does not provide us with the luxury of going along with things as they are. The new challenges must be met or our disabled people will, in the work they do, become, after all, second-class citizens. We could easily fall victim to a philosophy which dictates that there is no passion for improvement, no sense of urgency. "Don't worry. Ours is a noble cause. Think of the wonderful people whom we serve."

There still is, I fear, in many workshops servicing

the disabled, an abiding dislike for anything that smacks of salesmanship. We discovered (almost too late, as this story will tell), that we had made little real effort to find out what the markets were for our products and our services. Prior to that time, we thought that if we made it the way we always had, with sincerity of purpose and dedication for our own cause, we could sell the product on our own terms even if we failed to keep delivery dates or service promises, because ours was so noble a cause. Well, it didn't work. And this is the story that tells how, in finding this out the hard way, we almost failed entirely.

It's not easy when you're serving the cause of disabled people to think of cutting the price, to remember that high volume at reasonable profit is what makes the balance sheet blossom, that good salesmanship and marketing skills are as essential to an enterprise for the severely disabled as they are to any enterprise, and misuse of manpower cannot be condoned with us any more than it can in any good, well-run operation. To the urgency of proving that disabled people can work, must be added the drive to compete in a changing economy and an increasingly competitive industrial world. The competitive edge is as necessary for disabled people as it is for all people in industry. This is the story of what that simple but implacable arithmetic has meant to the extraordinary working force we call Abilities, Inc.

Henry Viscardi, Jr.

Albertson,
New York

# CONTENTS

# CONTENTS

## Part Three

## PLAN OF ACTION

# THE ABILITIES STORY

## PART ONE:

# *CRISIS*

# 1

## "The White House Calling . . ."

The place was Paris, the time October, 1961, a drizzling, cool Paris morning. In the quiet little hotel where my wife, Lucile, and I were staying, there was a knock at the door and a man's voice cried out excitedly in French. Although I speak French after a fashion, the words beyond the door were a meaningless half-hysterical jumble to me.

A moment later Lucile was out of the warm bed and opening the door. The night-concierge stood there, holding a piece of paper in his hand and informing her with obvious emotion, *"C'est la maison blanche, la maison blanche. . . ."*

To my semi-somnolent mind in the shivering half-light of morning the words I heard him telling her meant nothing. A white house, a white house. . . .

*"Le Président . . . le Président des États-Unis . . . Il vaus faut telephoner le Président . . . vous même . . . à la maison blanche"*—His voice was urgent *"immediatement, m'sieur. Immediatement."*

I heard my wife's voice across the room. "He's say-

ing you are to telephone the President immediately. At
the White House in Washington."

Call the White House? Why? My mind refused to
take it in. To add to my confusion, the entire hotel
seemed to be gathering in the corridor before our
door, as though they too knew that something extraordinary was happening.

She handed me the slip of paper the concierge had
given her. It was a hastily penciled message, apparently phoned in to the hotel from the cablegram office,
and was sent by my secretary at my office in America.

MEYER FELDMAN OF WHITE HOUSE ASKS I CABLE
YOU TO CALL HIM COLLECT NATIONAL EIGHT ONE
FOUR ONE FOUR RE PRESIDENTS SUGGESTION YOU
BECOME MEMBER OF PANEL ON MENTAL RETARDA-
TION HARRIET

I read the message a second time. It didn't make
sense. Although I was accustomed to working with the
physically disabled, the idea of working with the mentally retarded was a totally new thought.

Severely disabled physically myself—born without
legs—I had spent years helping other physically handicapped men and women. I had founded, in 1952, and
still head, Abilities, Inc., a work center that hires only
disabled workers, including those with the severest
disabilities. At our headquarters in Albertson, Long
Island, New York, these workers play a tremendously
productive role. Their efforts and the results they have
achieved have changed the attitude of industry
throughout the world toward the employment of disabled men and women.

I was in France, in fact, that chill fall of 1961, at the request of a group of men and women, headed by The Duchess Diane de Mouchy, to help them launch a French version of Abilities for their physically disabled. I had known the Duchess since the very early days of Abilities—"Our shoeless days in West Hempstead," we call them. She had come to see us to ask our advice on some plans she had had drawn up for a workshop to be staffed and operated by disabled persons, mostly paraplegics, at Ablon, a small village on the outskirts of Paris. It was to be the Abilities of France.

The French group already had some outside help. International Business Machines, for instance, was interested. But one of the reasons the Duchess had asked me to come over was to help them stir up the interest of the French people in the project. A speaking tour had been arranged in the major cities of France—first in Paris, then on to Lyons, Toulouse, Marseille, and other cities. The purpose, of course, was to awaken French industry to the largely untapped genius and productive potential of this unused labor force.

But the radiogram handed me by this jabbering Frenchman pertained to a quite different area of human rejection. It opened new doors to new needs, new problems, new questions—the answers to which I did not know in that cold French dawn.

Lucile was still standing at the door talking with the concierge. After a moment she turned to me and explained that the man had already read the message, that apparently he had awakened all the staff and most of the guests, and that everybody seemed to believe that I was supposed to call Mr. John F. Kennedy at the White House. Now all the concierge wanted was for me to give him the word to place the call to Mr. Kennedy.

I was, I remember, distinctly annoyed by this cable. Why me? Because I was legless and worked with other people with physical disabilities and understood their problems, why should anyone assume that my experience with them would make me any kind of authority on mentally retarded people?

Lucile, almost as excited as the concierge, suggested that I consider calling Washington at once. I replied that I had no intention of doing so.

"What do I know about this kind of problem?" I asked her. "Why do they want me on this panel anyway?"

Lucile, with her wifely intuition, made no answer, except to suggest that we get dressed and go downstairs to breakfast. There we were joined a little later by Jack Taylor, who was also with us on this mission of talking to the French business leaders about our rehabilitation employment techniques in America. A friend of many years, an authority in the field of disability, and a member of the Board of Directors of our Human Resources Center, Jack is also a close associate of the world-renowned Dr. Howard Rusk, Director of the New York University Institute of Rehabilitation Medicine.

The croissants and the *café au lait* did make the world seem a little more livable, and Lucile appeared to think it was safe to bring up the matter of the cablegram.

"Let's talk about the cable, Hank," she said. "The whole hotel is excited by it. I mean, this is the most exciting thing that's ever happened in this place—a cablegram from the White House! Asking you to call!" She hesitated. "What are you going to do about it?"

I said, very calmly, "I'm going to refuse."

For a moment she was shocked into silence. Then she said thoughtfully, "How, Hank? How do you refuse the President of the United States when he asks you to do something?"

Jack Taylor seemed a little startled at all this and Lucile began to explain to him what had happened. "Listen," he broke in, "I know the whole story. It was Dr. Rusk who suggested your name, Hank, because of your work in the field of employment of the disabled. I'm sorry—I just forget to tell you. But you can't refuse, Hank. You know Lucile's right. You can't."

I could understand how—in all the rush of the flight to Paris—Jack had forgotten to mention a minor thing like my being suggested for the new Presidential Committee on the retarded. And both he and Lucile were right when they said I could not refuse.

However, I was more than a little disturbed by this invitation to plunge into something of which I was no part and about which I knew virtually nothing. One of the things Abilities had always insisted upon was that its people, whatever their physical disabilities, be mentally sound.

But there was the challenge: one more area of need from which we could not turn away.

That was Thursday, the twelfth of October. On Saturday I flew back home. But before I left I received another cablegram:

THE FIRST MEETING OF THE PRESIDENTS PANEL ON MENTAL RETARDATION WILL BE HELD WEDNESDAY

OCTOBER EIGHTEEN AT NINETHIRTY AM. PLEASE PRE-
SENT THIS TELEGRAM AT NORTHWEST GATE OF THE
WHITE HOUSE

All the way on the flight back to America the
thought of this meeting in Washington was uppermost
in my mind, not because I was unused to working on
Presidential Commissions over the years, but because
of the implications of this new road on which I was
about to embark. For me, for Abilities, it meant more
than a meeting, more than a series of meetings on
empty words. Of this I was sure.

For the purposes of our Center run deep. Abilities,
Inc. was, and is, more than a business; it is a pilot
plant. From the beginning, our purpose was to show
the world that the disabled could work in industry,
could find uses for their abilities in real, not fabricated, work, could compete on almost even terms with
normal workers. We had taken on serious and important jobs, bidding with other companies, winning and
losing primarily on a basis of productivity, price controls, and quality standards. We had shown that we
could meet the needs of industry, which had, over the
years, ranged from producing electronic equipment
and components to putting together the complex wiring of airplane sections for major aircraft producers.
We had supplied these products to major aircraft companies and high-precision instrument manufacturers.

Our Work Center in Albertson employed more than
four hundred people, all disabled. And with other long-
range purposes we had also founded a research arm,
the Human Resources Center. We had also by that
time taken the initial steps toward building our

Human Resources School, to provide education for children so severely disabled that they were not able to attend any schools—and rarely, if ever, even allowed to leave their homes.

Gazing at the transatlantic darkness beyond the plane's window, I was aware of an anomaly in our situation. It would appear that we were, indeed, a triumphant operation. In large measure this was true. We welcomed visitors to our plant, and how often I have heard their exclamations: "What a wonderful thing you are doing, Mr. Viscardi! This is a tremendous operation, and everything is going in high gear. It is a real triumph."

But few of these people realized that there was another side of the Abilities story—the strictly non-sentimental business side. We had to accept the reality of the differences reflected in the severe disabilities of our people. To provide them with an opportunity, to work with the most severely disabled, to train workers who had no arms or legs, we had sought and been granted exemption from payment of Federal Income Tax and exemption from payment of Real Estate Taxes on our land and buildings.

This is an important advantage. It must be recognized, however, that it is offset by the length of time and degree of patience needed to make competitive, productive workers of our people. Some had been hospitalized or homebound for many years. They needed a long time and lots of ingenuity to become successful at electronics or banking operations.

Human Resources Center and the school needed support from Foundations and individuals, but from the beginning my whole goal—our whole goal—had been to prove that Abilities did not need to go hat-in-hand to anyone; we were not peddling pencils, this was not a new way of asking American industry to drop a few charity coins into our hat, our Work Center could be self-supporting.

We had asked no quarter, no dimes. But we faced many unanswered questions.

There was, at that time, no federal legislation such as now exists to provide funds for establishing workshops for the disabled. The results of our efforts and the efforts of others would make such legislation and assistance possible years later. To begin we had to borrow the funds and plan to "pay as you go," like any other business.

As the opportunity was presented in later years to obtain grants for research and demonstration projects under the Vocational Rehabilitation Administration and the New York State Division of Vocational Administration, we sought and received these grants. We still do.

If we had to do it over, I certainly would not incur long-range debt and would willingly accept grants for construction and equipment.

Hours later, as the plane approached New York, my mind turned from the problems of Abilities to the meeting at the White House. The thought of working with the retarded, while disturbing, was also challenging. It was a new field to explore. I had no idea what it might entail in terms of effort or responsibility, but I did know that its ramifications could present a jolting problem. Our own disabled might resent the whole idea of being in any way associated with these people, even remotely. Of course, I had no intention at all at that time of bringing the mentally retarded into Abilities itself.

Beyond this was the fact that we were in no position to take on anything new and untried, however worthy. Abilities was in financial difficulties. Business was in sharp decline everywhere at that time and nowhere more disastrous than in the industrial plants on Long Island, our major source of subcontracts. We had already been forced to cut back; I could only guess at what lay ahead.

Now, beside the grim business picture I was riding home to face, there was the coming conference at the White House.

But the fall days of 1961 were the bright new days of America's bright new President. There was so much about him that we did not know. When I reached the office I was briefed on the background leading to the formation of the President's new panel: Mr. Kennedy had a sister who was mentally retarded and one of the resolves he had made when he became President was to make a frontal attack on mental retardation in America. Thus he had leaned heavily on the advice of Dr. Howard Rusk, one of the leading forces in the rehabilitation of the disabled—and one of our close associates at Abilities, a board member and advisor.

When the President's aides showed Dr. Rusk the list of names originally selected for the panel, Rusk's first reaction was concern over the fact that the men chosen were all high-level scientists—sociologists, biologists, biochemists, physicists. Rusk advised, "I think you'd better get someone with practical experience to work on this thing with the others. The man I recommend is Hank Viscardi."

The cable I received in Paris was the result of President Kennedy's affirmative response to that suggestion.

When I arrived in Washington Wednesday morning, I was surprised to learn that not only were the panelists assembling at the White House, but the first actual panel sessions were also to be held there. I had served on Presidential Commissions as far back as F.D.R., and through Truman and Eisenhower, but the only time we ever got into the White House was for our initial reception or an opening handshake by the President—never for an actual work session. This, I was informed, was going to be different.

It was a gathering of learned men and women into which I entered. Among them, Nobel Prize winners. The chairman was Dr. Leonard Mayo, Director of the Association for the Aid of Crippled Children. As the discussion progressed, however, I began to realize that I could contribute little if this panel was concerned only with the treatment, cure, and prevention of mental retardation, but not at all with what to do about millions of mentally retarded individuals presently trying to find better jobs than raking leaves, picking up bits of paper along the city streets, or vegetating in institutions or at home in the shadows on the back porch.

This first meeting was truly high-level. It included President Kennedy's sister, Eunice, and her husband R. Sargent Shriver, later head of the Peace Corps and the Anti-Poverty program, Secretary of Labor Arthur J. Goldberg, and Abraham A. Ribicoff, Secretary of Health, Education and Welfare.

I listened attentively to what was primarily a discussion of the effects of mental retardation on the individual and on society, and a report on its symptoms and the techniques used in diagnosis and treatment. When it came my turn to speak, I said frankly that I was confused and disturbed, because the problem did not, in my view, concern only possible future treatment and prevention. We had, in addition, the immediate problem of what to do for the more than five million retarded people in the United States, here and now.

"If the sole purpose of this panel," I said, "is to find the cure and prevention of retardation, I can contribute nothing. I am not a scientist. I don't fully understand genetics or biochemistry. That part is certainly important, but there are other aspects that should not be forgotten or pushed aside."

"It seems to me," I continued, "that we should find a way to evaluate these people; find ways to determine those who are educable and their employment potential; determine how they might best be employed, where, and under what conditions, and then develop ways of training them for useful work. It had been my hope that this panel would devote some of its deliberations to this end."

As I stood there in the silence I was aware that they knew who I was, so to strengthen my point I told them a little about Abilities; how hard we had worked to change the attitude of industry in general to the employment potentials of the physically disabled. I described the wide variety of severe disabilities our people had, and the even wider variety of abilities and skills they brought to our strictly-business, competitive production lines.

But I had also, since the arrival of that message at our Paris hotel, been giving the question of the retarded much thought. And I had given close attention to the direction the talk had followed this morning in Washington.

As I looked around the gathering, I had the feeling that I was not making the contribution expected of me.

I felt that I was not making myself really understood. I was trying to say something I understood from my work with the disabled; the hunger of all people for productivity, for fulfillment. Yet putting all this meaning into words for these learned men was not that easy. I had said what I had to say, but I did not think I had reached them with my words.

Moments later, President Kennedy joined us. He talked briefly, but I felt brilliantly, on the subject of the retarded and what could and should be done for them. In the Rose Garden outside, to which we adjourned for newsreels and photographs, the President talked to the press about this panel he was setting up as a first step in a national attack on mental retardation.

It was an interesting, exciting moment, as the brilliant young President, standing before the cameras with the group around him, cited the statistics and described the vast scope of the problem, the need of salvaging these people for themselves and for society.

As the President finished his talk, I was standing about two persons away from him, beside the panel chairman, Dr. Mayo. Turning from the newsmen, Mr. Kennedy asked Dr. Mayo, quite unexpectedly, "How

long do you think it will take this panel to come up
with a report and specific recommendations for action
by Congress?"

It was a slightly unfair question to ask the chairman
of a panel whose first session had begun only two or
three hours earlier, but after a brief pause Dr. Mayo
was ready with an answer! "I think we can do this in
about a year, Mr. President."

Kennedy's bushy eyebrows came together in a sudden hint of mild concern. Secretary of Labor Goldberg, standing beside the President, seemed to sense
his attitude and said, "Mr. President, during the meeting Hank Viscardi made some mention of the great
work that's been done at Abilities and I am confident
that before a year is over we'll have a program of
action operating out there."

This bit of information was, I may say, news to me.
My mention of our work with the disabled had been a
brief one. I had certainly presented no specific plan of
action involving Abilities with the mentally retarded.
Nor did I have any in mind.

The President seemed gratified at Goldberg's statement. I am certain at the time that he didn't really
know what the answer fully meant, but looked at me
and smiled.

The picture-taking was over. President Kennedy
was leaving the group. But before Secretary Goldberg
left I managed to get in a quick question.

"I was delighted with your comment to the President, Mr. Secretary," I said. "But could you perhaps
be more specific?"

The Secretary put his arm around my shoulders.
"You'll figure out the details. I only opened the door.

You'll take care of the rest. I'm not at all worried and neither is the President."

But *I* was, although there was no time to dwell on it.

The reception, later in the afternoon, was a delight. So was an inner tour of the White House.

The excursion provided a charming, informal social interlude for the group. At the reception, Eunice Shriver came up to me. "The President," she said, "was very pleased with our report to him on the remarks you made during the meeting and he's asked me to find out more specifically what you plan to do."

I had no answer. Things had moved too fast. As I hedged, Mrs. Shriver, a charming and impetuous lady, went on. "I'd like to come out and see Abilities."

Part of the picture became clear when she said that. Eunice Shriver had an assignment: it was mental retardation. We, that is, Abilities, were in it.

"You remember the hero of *Harvey?*" I said quickly. "If anyone ever said to the hero, 'I'd like to buy you a drink,' he always said, 'When?' And if anybody ever said to him, 'What can I do for you?' he always said, 'What do you have in mind?'"

Mrs. Shriver laughed. "Obviously, you want to know when." She called to her secretary, who came over carrying Mrs. Shriver's engagement book. "Wednesday of next week," the President's sister said, after glancing at the pages.

I was delighted. Whatever else I might have planned for Wednesday was automatically canceled.

"You can pick me up in New York," Mrs. Shriver said. "I'll be staying at the Kennedy apartment."

But the plans of Presidents and their entourages frequently shift, so later this date was moved to the following week, between an appointment at Hattie Carnegie's, where she would be having her hair done, and a United Nations dinner, at which she would represent the President.

I sent our one-handed chauffeur, Johnny, with the station wagon to pick her up at Hattie Carnegie's. Some time later Johnny telephoned.

"The lady sent out word she won't be done with her hair till after three," he said.

"That's too late, Johnny," I told him. "Tell her we close at four-fifteen. Explain that she's got to see the place with the people here, not deserted. You go in there and tell her."

"Go in there?" Johnny sounded shocked. "I can't go in there, boss. I don't have a poodle." He paused. Then he added, "There isn't a lady going in there the last hour didn't have a poodle."

But word did get to her, through Wally Tudor, a Vice President of Sears, who had gone along to escort her to the plant.

A few minutes later Johnny called back. "Okay, boss. We got the lady out from under the dryer. We're on our way."

"On our way," I repeated silently as I hung up. On our way to what?

The President's concern for, and response to, the problem of the retarded was suddenly enveloping me and Abilities and our whole operation, as we in turn responded to a request, a need, from the chief executive of the United States.

What we could do and how we would do it, I did

not know. But it was in keeping with the way Abilities functioned. We could never turn away from the need of people, for our prime reason for existence was the need of people, human beings, heretofore the disabled in body. Now perhaps the mind.

One thing I did know was that Abilities could not do it alone. We would have to have help, training research funds of some kind, to support any original pilot operation, or even preliminary studies. Training techniques, evaluation criteria, work-simplification methods and devices were needed. On our part it would require a costly investment of time, energy, and effort. Where would it all come from—this tremendous expenditure that lay ahead if we were to go forward, as it now appeared certain we would, even though the details were still to be worked out? The problem was typical of our whole history from the beginning.

Such precedent had been set since we were already operating under a Vocational Rehabilitation Administration grant for our telemetry research.

At the same moment I was contemplating what could be done for the mentally retarded, Abilities was facing a near depression on Long Island. Electronic and aircraft industries and related enterprises were our most important customers; without them we could not exist twenty-four hours. At this time—with the Korean War and its needs long since over—industrial concerns were undergoing severe retrenchment, particularly those on Long Island. They were laying off workers, cutting back on subcontracting and everywhere else they could, in an effort to keep operating at all. I did not have to be much of a seer to look into Abilities' immediate future and see the complications if we were to launch Project MR. Our board was going to tell me that we were already in a life-and-death struggle to hold on to what we had; it was no time to start something new and uncertain, need or no need; we had to be practical, realistic.

All the questions would come tumbling out. Haven't we proved enough, with the disabled? Don't we have enough trouble meeting all the debts Abilities already has, especially now when business is badly off and orders are not coming in? How can you mix the retarded and the physically handicapped together anyway? And the last final challenge: What do *you* know about the retarded?

All this ran through my mind as I waited for Johnny to arrive with Mrs. Shriver on her mission to see Abilities and to talk about how it could be related to a bright new program for the mentally retarded.

I was overwhelmed by the illogic of the situation. It was a preposterous, impossible moment as I sat there waiting for the President's sister to arrive from Hattie Carnegie's.

## 2

### *Free Enterprise For Whom?*

She had her hair and the curlers hidden by a lovely scarf. I greeted her at the entrance.

"What would you have done if I'd had photographers here?"

With the most gracious of smiles, she answered that she might have become violent.

With that we started on our late-afternoon tour of Abilities.

Even with our reduced staff, the place was throbbing with activity. As we passed the work benches, I explained the assorted operations we engaged in to fulfill our subcontracts, stopping here and there to point up some delicate procedure, some intricate manipulation, as the workers went about their jobs. Mrs. Shriver's questions revealed not only her interest, but an unusual understanding of the complexities of such electronic operations as the assembly of airplane wiring units—harness and cable operations as they are called.

As the visitor walks along the long wide aisles of

production, he forgets that this is a work center for the disabled. There are wheelchairs, yes; crutches and canes, artificial limbs and sundry braces—whatever is needed for the legless, the armless, the handless, the blind, or any other of a hundred varieties of disability. But these are not sick people; this is no hospital, no clinic. Abilities has no relationship to doctors or depression or sadness; it is a pulsating place of production and achievement and, to these workers, a fulfillment.

As Eunice Shriver walked with me through the aisles, observing and talking with our people, she made no attempt to conceal her feelings. Her eyes and her voice expressed her enthusiasm. When we reached my office, she turned quickly to what was closest to her heart—mental retardation.

"Now when do we get started bringing in the mentally retarded?" she asked eagerly.

Here was the paradox I could not escape. We were laying off workers—people who needed their jobs more desperately than most because it was so hard for them to find others. But we had to take the ups and downs, we had no choice. On the other side of the paradox was Mrs. Shriver asking me to hire new workers, mentally retarded people of whose compensative working potentials no one in the world at that time had any real knowledge.

The electronics industry from which we got so much of our work was hard hit. Republic Aircraft was in serious trouble. Sperry Gyroscope had cut back heavily responding to government cutbacks. We—Abilities—despite the glittering façade, were in a desperate situation.

I told Mrs. Shriver it was not quite that easy, that automatic, this idea of putting the mentally retarded to work in Abilities. It was after all a complex competitive environment, not fabricated work. Although I had already accepted in my mind the new concept that these people should be a part of our concern (after all, the retarded were as much a part of the disabled as the legless, the armless, the sightless), they presented new problems.

"I think we can prove that the MR's can do a variety of operations," I told Mrs. Shriver, "but the techniques have to be worked out. This has to be supported. It will have to have some kind of Federal or private foundation support. A new approach to job research and training programs will be necessary. We can't just find them jobs by snapping our fingers and throwing other people out of work to do it."

I didn't go into the whole picture, but I was sure she understood.

"No, of course not," she said. "But there's a meeting of the panel in Baltimore next week and we'll work it out. I'll see you there."

We shook hands, and the smiling lady hurried off to get ready to represent the President at the United Nations dinner.

The meeting in Baltimore, at one of the hotels near Johns Hopkins University, was once again mostly made up of professionals, social scientists, doctors, pediatricians, physicists, and geneticists talking about their problems: the causes and possible avenues of prevention of retardation. It was enlightening and helpful. When the meeting was over, the Shrivers asked me to have a cup of coffee with them. "We want to talk, Hank," Mrs. Shriver said.

Over the coffee cups, Sargent Shriver said with all his friendly enthusiasm, "Listen, what have you done since you made those suggestions in the White House?"

I was taken aback. I said, "I haven't done much except to think about it."

Impatiently Shriver broke in, "Look, it's a good idea. But when do we get started?"

"Mr. Shriver," I said, "it's not that easy. We're busy fighting a diminishing workload up in Long Island. We're going to have to lay off a lot of disabled people; we've laid off a lot already. We don't have the kind of resources to crank in something as new and exotic as this."

It was as basic and realistic as that.

"We are not seeking charity, Mr. Shriver," I went on. "We are trying to operate in a business-like fashion. If part of our end-product is fulfilled people—that is one of our chief goals—we perform a service. Service is a part of the end product of any business. But to perform a service, even we must first be solvent."

Shriver was watching with great earnestness, but made no attempt to answer. Nor did his wife. After a second, I continued more quietly. "In a competitive environment such as ours the retarded represent a new challenge. One relatively unknown. I believe that work can be simplified and training methods devised so that even with limited minds they can be trained to become electronic technicians or bank clerks. But work simplification techniques and training methods must be devised.

"I have in mind an audio-visual method of training, using colored slides and taped instruction which is simplified and repetitive. The same approach as teaching a child to do a complex task. Simplify it by breaking it down; make it attractive with colored slides and repeat it endlessly."

I looked at them both. "But they'll need jobs, work which they can do after they are trained. If we're going to get started, somebody's going to have to give us some funds for training and research and some help to get business and a new mix in the workload."

This tall man beside me, already one of the most important forces in our social and economic structure, suddenly grinned. "Why didn't you tell me?" he asked. "I'll call you tomorrow."

The next day he telephoned me to say I had an appointment with Mary Switzer, Commissioner of Vocational Rehabilitation in the Department of Health, Education and Welfare. Mary Switzer is an old friend. We had worked with her associates, Dr. Jim Garrett and Dr. Bill Usdane before. They believed in us and had already supported our research and demonstration projects. The result was that they agreed to provide funds: a research and demonstration grant to develop techniques for training the mentally retarded in competitive industry. The funds would be there, and any other assistance they could give, they said, but we had to come up with the project protocol and the training techniques. The grant request would be submitted to their Council for approval. The work was not to be the kind of thing the mentally retarded had done traditionally—being messengers, stacking one box on top of another. They were to be given real jobs. Work demanding skills and competency at a relatively high clerical level and as electronic technicians.

This, after all, is what I had proposed and what we

had to come up with to qualify for funds from Washington.

On my return to New York, I began to realize how deeply I had become involved in this new challenge, even as I was trying to figure out what to do about our own problems. There was the psychological problem too —the reaction of the workers in our plant when they learned that we were going to bring in people whose mental capabilities didn't reach normal levels.

During this period of great concern, I recall sitting in my office late one sunny afternoon. As I watched the workers leaving, driving off in their own cars (almost all of our workers, even the armless, drive their own cars), I realized the double crisis we were facing. On one hand there was our desperate economic situation; on the other, the approaching change in policy. We were about to extend our direction, to reach out to the mentally retarded and bring them into out work program. It was a difficult, indeed almost dangerous, step. Yet we could not turn from it. It was our history. It had always been our history, from our first starving days in an empty garage in a place called West Hempstead. Added to this was the doubt whether the retarded could be trained to do our complex work. I couldn't remember ever having talked to one. In fact, it occurred to me I had never seen one or if I had, I was unaware of it.

An image that frequently comes to my mind seems to symbolize those beginnings—the memory of a moment, the image of a man who was to become one of my closest friends and business associates, and one of the top executives of Abilities.

That moment was long before there was any vast,

sprawling Work Center employing hundreds of disabled workers at its benches—an Abilities being copied throughout the world; before the establishment of the Human Resources Center with its research projects and a staff constantly seeking new ways to understand, and new techniques to help solve the problems of the disabled in order to use their potentials most effectively. And long before we built our unique Human Resources School, designed to meet educational needs of the severely disabled child.

It was also long, long before the President of the United States had sent word that the country needed us and our plant to include the problem few others had dared to touch: a new approach for the mentally retarded in competitive industry.

But the image was still sharp in my mind—the image of a man with little paralyzed legs sitting in a homemade wheelchair, sweeping a floor.

As Art Nierenberg had put it then, I was the logical one to get the ball rolling on the daring new idea that the handicapped—even the most severely handicapped—had the abilities required to operate a successful work center, supporting itself out of earnings and on a business-like basis.

At that time I was the director of J.O.B.—Just One Break—an organization set up with the aid of Dr. Howard Rusk and Bernard Baruch to find jobs for the disabled. In the course of this work, quite apart from my own personal experiences, I had had to face the difficulties which the disabled meet in industry. I have told this story in other books, the story of the turndowns, the lack of understanding by industry in those days. Art had come to me looking for a job and I had told him my idea of starting such an operation.

Art Nierenberg was then only twenty-four years old, with a wife, a child, a fine mind, and skilled hands, particularly in jewelry-making and now in electronics. Art had faith that I could do this thing. He was willing to give up his electronic job in a major company to come with me. It was a job I had found for him. And Art would not let the project stay in the idea state; he kept at me, nagging me. When and where was I going to launch this Abilities?

I tried to sound out a few people about it. We held some meetings with those I managed to interest. But nothing tangible developed. It was still a dream, and Art and I would go home, I on my artificial limbs back to my lovely wife and daughters, Art back to his family.

Finally, I decided someone had to take the risk, the first step. With a few hundred dollars I rented a garage on a month-to-month basis. I had little left after I had paid the first month's rent. But we had a place. Now all we needed were jobs, some machinery, benches, some financing.

I did have our first employee, the plant manager, Art Nierenberg. Now as I sat in the sunlight some ten years later, I could see him in my mind, alone in that empty barn-like building, sweeping the floor—in those days we had an empty garage, one broom, a staff of two, and no orders to fill.

The story of this book is a business story. It is not about disabled people, "manufactured" work, pity, tears, pathos. It is a story of inventories, contracts, and subcontracts, of creating products and reaching markets, of facing the new competitive challenge—a challenge faced by disabled people who, rightly or wrongly, asked no quarter, no dimes in any held-out hat. They asked only a chance to work, to compete, with whatever abilities they could muster. A quality product would be delivered on time and at a fair price to a select customer in a sophisticated market. No rug-weaving or basket-making for us.

It is a business story in that it has special meaning to all who believe in individual freedom and equality of opportunity to compete in the open marketplace, even for individuals others think of as crippled. For what has happened, and still happens at Abilities and Human Resources, touches all of us, all Americans—whole, normal, average—and especially the pounding industrial complex of the country.

So we began, back in 1952, with the help of a few friends and associates. I have to acknowledge at once that in those days neither Art nor I was in any sense a businessman. Art, at least, had some experience. He had already started and lost a business. Borrowing six thousand dollars from his father, he had set up a furniture business, but was clobbered early in the game when some fast-talking merchandisers sold him on the idea of making a certain kind of rocking-chair. He made the chairs, in fact he made so many of them he didn't have enough money to support his inventory, so he went under. It wasn't a promising experience, to be sure, but at least Art had been through the wringer and knew what business was like.

I had never started a business. I'd worked for big companies, Mutual Broadcasting System, where I'd been in sports and special events, and Burlington Mills, where I'd been personnel director. But I knew that if we could learn the ground rules, even if we had to figure them out ourselves, we could succeed in bringing handicapped people into productive roles in industry. I was also convinced that if we didn't do this, the disabled would continue to be hopeless and jobless.

Things are greatly changed because of the success of this and similar ventures, but in 1952 the whole field of industrial employment for the disabled was an untried area, full of questions without answers. These questions I kept to myself. Before this, as director of J.O.B., I had been working day and night, beating the industrial bushes to get jobs for these thousands of disabled men and women seeking employment. The going was slow, the pickings meager. The average answer of the average company president was, "Show me."

Show me—what? Well, what these people could do. Show me that the disabled could do a day's work. During our early days when I first began to try to get jobs for Abilities, we coined an expression to describe the attitude of industry to the disabled at that time: "The only thing they think we're good for is pasting feathers on the back ends of ducks on Easter cards."

In the area of personnel administration, I did have background. I'd trained for it and I worked at industrial relations. One thing I knew was that there were no ground rules in dealing with the question of employment for the disabled. No one had yet designed a technique for determining their potentials. Physical requirements for jobs were rigid. A typist had to pass a physical equal to a distance runner. No one had made an honest-to-God job evaluation as to who could or could not do a specific job. The only thing then going for them on an extensive scale were the Goodwill Industries and sheltered workshops. Someone had to draw new ground rules, had to have the experience, had to build the showcase, put on a demonstration that people could look at.

To fill up that immense empty garage seemed a tremendous task. (Actually, we had only twenty-four-hundred square feet, but at the time it appeared larger than the ninety-three-thousand square feet we have in our Abilities operation today.) There were no precedents to follow, nothing like it had ever before been attempted, what we were doing was unique.

But we had faith in it and people helped us, people who believed in it as we did. At a meeting at the Garden City Hotel, Arthur Roth, president of the Franklin National Bank, demonstrated his faith in a very tangible way: he offered to lend us, as a start, four thousand dollars, if we could match that amount from other sources. I went to friends and we raised the money. We had eight thousand dollars and we were in business.

Abilities, Inc., was established as a non-profit corporation because there would be no profits; every cent of earnings, above costs and salaries, would be plowed back into research and expansion for the benefit of disabled people. Tax exemption was requested and granted on the grounds that we would make wage earners and taxpayers out of the disabled who were now supported by others. This was the one concession we had to make, the realistic margin, the edge, without which we had no chance to compete. We had the problem of developing training techniques and new methods of performing almost any job. Risks had to be taken with persons considered too sick to work, cardiacs, amputees, paraplegics. At the start, each worker was a special case, each disability a technical problem to be solved. A whole new employment procedure remained to be evolved.

For our opening venture we could have raised more than eight thousand dollars if we had tried. But Joseph Landow, who became our treasurer and who at that time was recommended to us by Arthur Roth, didn't think more was advisable. "If you don't have it," he said, "if you have to work close to the line, you'll be more careful. You won't throw money out the window. You'll watch every cent. At the beginning of any business venture that's good. There's something about starting with a very small sum that gives people a driving force to go forward."

With the money in hand, the next thing we needed was jobs. The first to come in was for the company next door, a manufacturer of model aircraft for children. Abilities was to make parts for a model plane assembly—for kids! It was a long way from where we were headed, but it was a start. At least we were in the aircraft business. Art went out and borrowed a second-hand drawing board and set to work drafting plans for the plane—plans which ultimately were dropped because the model firm went out of business.

Next we contemplated a mail-order service. We would set up and operate folding, stamping, and sealing machines for a mail-order house. I was furious when the fellow turned us down. Then I realized my mistake: we weren't asking for favors. If he didn't want us in, he didn't want us. Next case!

Our first real break came from an electronics firm that was loaded with orders for the Korean War effort. They gave us an order for three hundred and forty sets of "harnesses," for the wiring system of Saberjet fighters. The planes were badly needed at the front and all the regular manufacturers were busy on other war contracts. To our novice eyes, the fee was a small fortune: eighteen hundred and seventy dollars!

We began to put together our first office force and to bring in our first machines, to set up our first work benches. Art took care of the benches, seeing that they were spaced so our people could get through and around them on crutches, in wheelchairs, or by whatever means of locomotion they used.

"Staff" came in slowly. One boy on crutches—both legs badly crippled, one arm partially, little education, less job experience. He'd held two jobs, each for one week. Another "staffer" was a man injured in World War II, paralyzed from the waist down. He was a skilled craftsman with precision tools, but nobody would give him a job. A third was a man who had lost an arm and a leg in a construction accident. And Art, of course, in his wheelchair. Art was foreman of this strange conglomeration. All told, we had a working force of four men with five good arms and one good leg.

From the date of the receipt of this first contract, we were on our road. We were a new idea, a novelty, an exciting innovation. Moreover, there were orders to be filled, for in these days of manpower shortage, we offered an answer to people who needed small jobs done that bigger concerns had no time for.

We hired a part-time secretary, an amputee, Florence, on a three-days-a-week basis. We got machinery —begged, borrowed, or bought—as needs required. We began to make printed circuits, a complex wiring mechanism, for some of the big companies in electronics. Additional jobs, some large, some small, were subcontracted to us from aircraft companies.

Sperry Gyroscope Co. and others from whom we obtained work helped out. Organization became a major problem. We had to devise techniques for getting the work done, accurately and on time, in the light of the individual disabilities of the personnel available to do a particular job.

More than this was required. As work volume increased, so did industrial problems. In little ways at first, but they had to be faced. Purchasing of materials, work-flow methods to keep the workers supplied, setting prices, inspection and quality control, shipping and receiving, salary rates, fringe benefits, insurance and all the things we had said we could do in our brave new competitive world.

Today all of these procedures are so well worked out that it is difficult to recall the myriad problems of 1952. These covered such elementary things as teaching workers how to sit at benches; determining how high the benches should be and where they should be; how wide to make the aisles, how to set up lavatories, how to train these new workers. How, for instance, does a man with steel hooks for hands learn to solder?

We had problems in regard to insurance. The companies were worried about safety. We had no records of safety, of course, no records period. Then there was concern about what insurance calls compensation liability—injuries from accidents that occur in factories whether they are manned by able or disabled people.

None of these worries exists in quite the same fashion today because the operation has become routine. Our records show an extraordinary safety history, far better than that of the average industrial plant. The insurance people have discovered that the worker with one hand is more careful than those of us who have two.

The work flowed in. We were soon hustling not only to get jobs but to get workers to perform them. In a few months we had twenty employees, then forty, then over sixty. Legless, blind, paralyzed, the war-injured—the whole sweep of disabilities was represented in our work staff. People who heretofore had been turned down for jobs were suddenly part of a new, exciting adventure.

In terms of business there was so much that we did not know. But it did not matter to us. We were a success. We were competing in industry, we were about to show the world what we could do. From top management to the newest armless worker at the bench, we believed in ourselves.

## 3

## *Cold Facts*

A business is more than figures and merchandise, profits and losses; a business includes people. In our operation, it was first of all people. And we could not always predetermine or control the direction this human element would take.

For instance, a young boy came into Abilities, a youth who had a brilliant mind and high work-potential, but on the surface he appeared to be a twisted spastic who could not work or speak as others do. For years he had worked on and off as a messenger, then he heard of Abilities and applied for a job. We trained him and we opened up a whole new horizon by putting him to work on an electronics product.

But we did not anticipate that he would fall in love with one of our workers, a polio-paralyzed young lady who carried out her work assignments in a very busy wheelchair. It was a typical office romance with the usual office gossip and complications, the usual family discussions and concerns, followed by the ultimate wedding bells and a party by fellow workers for the newlyweds.

This was a normal office episode that has occurred many times over in the business world. So it happened to us at Abilities, among workers living lives like all other people in the world, hoping, loving, worrying, quarreling. And just as all others too, our people are ambitious, full of themselves and their dreams, at times frightened, as any normal person is, but each in his own way becoming, as every individual must, the sum total of his drives and efforts.

One of the cold facts we had to recognize at the outset was that we had to devise special techniques and training programs for specific jobs and disabilities. In those first days, industry had no such programs. We pioneered in finding techniques for teaching the disabled worker to use to the maximum whatever abilities he had. This meant developing and later formalizing and codifying techniques and training programs. The beginning was a time of trial and error, as we gradually developed procedures, methods of evaluation, training programs.

It was because we realized the basic necessity of continuous evaluation and training programs, and the expense they would entail, that we soon applied for tax-exempt status. Without that margin for research, an expansion program would have been impossible. Our workers were not cold statistics, but human beings who were learning not merely how to work and earn, but learning also how to live. There were not only romances and marriages, new homes and children, but other intimately personal benefits. Husbands and fathers regained purpose and standing in their own homes and families, because *they* were the bread-winners. We opened a cafeteria where they might gather socially because, quite obviously, our workers were not about to go out hunting a corner lunchroom. Our location was against this in any event. None were handy. There were recreation get-togethers, a bowling team. It was a new kind of social "outreach" many of them found for the first time.

We were a pilot operation, not only in products we turned out on the machines, but in the workers we turned out for the machines, as well. So I insisted from the start—and insist today—that the *people* at Abilities were our major product, a product which in one highly significant sense we were selling to the world: the potential of our workers.

Because of the publicity we received, industry was awakening to what our people could do on an assembly line. That industry has bought what we have to offer is apparent from the fact that in periods of manpower shortage we find ourselves in a highly competitive position trying to hold on to our trained supervisors and skilled workers, who are often hired away by one or another of the larger industrial plants. In one sense, we do not mind the loss; it is further proof of what the training and work program of Abilities means. Whereas in the past, few of the severely physically disabled could not even beg a job, now they are being sought, particularly after some training and actual experience on the line.

Sometimes, I wondered if most of industry would ever fully understand just how much we, the disabled, could do, how large a role we could play. We were only a few hundred human beings. There were millions more—fifteen percent of the nation. How much had we done to open the doors of industry to this tremendous, but largely neglected and rejected, potential?

I still have conflicting ideas on this area of our story —how far we have been able to make inroads. That we have made some, in cooperation with great industries, agencies, and individuals, cannot be denied. But it is still a beginning. All the battles have not yet been won. Back in those early days, the issues had not even been joined; many of the causes of conflict, many of the operational problems, were not recognized or understood.

I recall our financial advisor, Joe Landow, talking at board meetings in the early days of Abilities. We held those meetings in the garage, at night, in an improvised "board room" made up of work tables pulled together. We had brought onto our board a number of distinguished businessmen and other persons interested in rehabilitation problems. But much of the discussion at the board meetings consisted of the hard arithmetic of our production activities. In the midst of our seeming success, Joe expressed concern. "Yes," he said, "we have contracts. Sperry Gyroscope and Republic and others are feeding us work. But what happens if the well runs dry, if the prime companies who subcontract to us find their workload cut back? Where do we go then?"

Joe cited another point that worried him—and me. "Ninety-eight percent of all the work we get, Hank brings in personally. That's good but it is also dangerous. What if something happens to Hank? Where would we be? Our whole business could collapse overnight if we lost Hank through sickness, accident . . . anything."

These were serious points. Much of our work came from defense contracts. We were helping America halt communism in Korea. But what would we do when we won, which we all knew was not many months away? We all deeply prayed for the war to be over, not only because it would mean that we had stopped another communist aggression, but also because it would put an end to the drain on American lives. "Defense business is short-term business, no matter what," Landow would say. "Only by balanced long-range and short-range business, carefully evolved, can we maintain ourselves on an even keel."

But to go back for a moment to our beginnings— we had no time then for long-range concepts. We were too busy reaching out in our new unprecedented triumphs.

In 1953-54 the defense budgets were still high and they would continue even after the fighting in Korea was completely over. But in the up-and-down world of war and the defense against possible war, the downward trend did not begin when the last gun was fired and the peace terms established. Industry still rolled on. We now had fifty to sixty workers. As we took on new jobs to meet new bills, we ran into the increasing problems of any business in a state of growing too swiftly. Each new order required materials, and these had to be purchased from cash reserves or on short-term loans at required interest rates.

Often we would not be paid even on delivery, but only upon final acceptance of our product, and that could be months later. In the meantime, Abilities had to pay for the materials and the labor, regardless. Our expenses were growing with the workload. The problems of borrowing, short-term or long-term, also were growing.

When we began to get the idea of building the new plant at Albertson, with space enough to do ten times the production of the garage, we faced the next step, the money for the new building.

From the start, our great problem in Abilities was financing—financing at the correct level; not over-financing and wasting funds, but not underfinancing either. The truth was, we were growing so fast in the beginning that we had to have more space, more equipment, more workers, more research. All this took money. To make it, we couldn't be too choosy about the jobs we took. Anything we got into the shop was that much more business, whether it was for model planes or war planes. Any customer was a friend if the job was at all possible. With this attitude, you can lose too; you may get the job nobody else wants to risk trying. In those beginning years, we took whatever we could get, no matter what it was. Some we liked and some we didn't. We were in the position of a doctor or lawyer who at the start of his practice takes any case he can see on the horizon, and if he doesn't know how to handle it, he finds out. That's part of the learning process and it's the best thing at that stage for a man or a business. Even one like ours.

When we started to make printed circuits, for instance, our board chairman, industrialist Preston Bassett, told us that his firm was working on similar jobs. "The people in our electronics shop know a lot about these print circuits but they still present difficulties. But I think our Abilities people can handle these problems and we'll help if we can."

The printed circuit, which in those days was a rela-

tively new development, became one of our early spe-
cialities. It, too, will be made obsolete by new techniques now being perfected. In effect, it is a modern
replacement for hand-strung wiring. Formerly, strands
of copper wire, insulated or not, were strung between
points to allow current to flow. This required soldering
or some other means of fastening the wires, plus insulation at any points where other connections
crossed. In the modern printed circuit, instead of
actual wiring, a strip of copper is printed (just the
same as an ink line is printed) on a flat "wafer"
which is an insulator. Another copper connection can
be printed on the other side of the wafer. None of this
requires stringing of wires; the components are sol-
dered on. The entire board is dipped into a solder bath
after the components are fastened. This completes the
circuit. By this time-saving technique, once the master
wafer is designed, innumerable copies can be run off
on a "printing press" using copper lines instead of ink
lines.

What we found in practice was that our people,
once the methodology was worked out, excelled the
non-disabled in many instances. For one thing, they
had developed patience over long years of enforced
sedentary life. Further, the disabled worker, who may
be in a wheelchair or on crutches or in some other way
have little or no mobility, gives more of his attention
over longer periods of time than can the non-disabled.
The disabled man knows that his work bench is where
he stays; he can't get away from it as often as the non-
disabled. His attention, his interest, and his effort center on the assignment; it becomes his escape, his creative outlet, in many cases the heart of his world.

When Art Nierenberg hired our first blind worker,

he found the problem of teaching the man to handle a wirewinding operation. In the course of the instruction, Art noticed the man was wearing a Braille watch, and he recalled how aviators used the time-piece dial to indicate directions such as: "Enemy planes at three o'clock."

Art decided to use the same device. "You bring the wire here, to three o'clock," he said. "And you take it across to eight o'clock." And the sightless man's fingers moved from three o'clock to eight. . . .

Our staff grew in those days from fifty to more than a hundred. Despite the fact that we were subcontracting, that there was always the danger of a sudden cancellation, that we had to feel our way on every new job, our success continued. Despite the warnings and alarms we all expressed from time to time, the worries that I lay awake with in the long nights, our gross figures mounted. But I knew we could not be content to serve as an outlet for these relatively few disabled people when there were millions more who needed such help.

Abilities had to become more. It had to become a national center for the study of the problems of the disabled. This was where the idea of expansion had begun in the late 1950's. We called a board meeting to discuss the idea. In the give-and-take of this discussion, my own ideas began to crystallize. How could we use our human resources most effectively? To determine this, we needed a research center where the problems of the disabled would be constantly explored. And we needed a new place in which to establish new

buildings. Abilities, a research center and a workshop
. . . and some day . . . the school.

There were meetings with the board, with interested
outsiders, with Arthur Roth, the banker. It was finally
agreed that we had to take the step, because we could
not let Abilities and its meanings and program stand
still. We would do it as we had done all the rest. To
raise money, we would issue some kind of bond, it was
agreed. When one board member asked Roth who
would handle the debentures, his answer was, "Well, I
assume it will be our bank—the Franklin National. I
can't think of a sounder investment in America today."
But sound banking procedures were followed.
Franklin assumed no liability for the debentures;
the liability was ours. The debentures were a preferred
risk as to creditors except for the mortgage on the
physical plant and property.

Because we were disabled, the world outside had
seen only the magic, the almost miraculous thing that
was developing: this buzzing industrial activity of
people whom the world usually shunned, usually kept
out of the mainstreams of business activity and too
often treated with pity. To the public, our expansion
program seemed only one more logical step.

It was far more than that to us. It was a difficult,
even rash, action.

I didn't quite comprehend the financial terminology, but I gathered it was something between a bond
and a stock with a dash of trust and faith in what we
had done and would do. Perhaps these were the best
things we had to offer.

Perhaps, too, it was no way to run an airline or an
industrial work center. But it was the only way we had

open to us. In a world of free enterprise, you have to use whatever methods present themselves.

So we began on two fronts: on the one, to borrow money for a whole new outreach; on the other, to find a site and begin to build.

In Albertson, Long Island, we had found a piece of open, level land, with a brook and woods nearby. There was space for buildings and for expansion; grounds for recreation; water, trees, and greenery. The owner, the late real-estate man Jacob Gellman, was asking ninety thousand dollars for it. The price was fair. Gellman was a tough businessman; he didn't want to come to see our plant in West Hempstead, he didn't want his sound business judgment to be influenced. We talked back and forth. Ultimately, he called me up and said, "Okay, Hank, I'll make the price one hundred thousand dollars instead of ninety. I'll sell you half of the acreage for sixty thousand and give you the forty-thousand-dollar half as a contribution."

We were not begging or asking for sympathy. But we could use this kind of help. I could hear in Gellman's voice the warmth of the man. I made a fast decision.

"Could you do it in two installments?" I asked. "You know, you might get better tax deduction if you spread the gift over two years."

Gellman laughed and told me that perhaps I ought to be working in his office.

He may have been right, for I went out and sold those debentures; something like three-hundred-thousand-dollars worth of them. Later, we raised mortgage money to cover the rest of the costs. A handful of neighbors in Albertson protested our plans, but they failed to file their appeal in time and we were able to go ahead and build.

The building that went up on the lot was designed specifically for the needs of a work center staffed by the disabled. Everything had to be custom-made— ramps instead of stairs, wide, easily negotiable corridors and aisles, special lavatories and toilet facilities, water coolers with faucets at both stand-up and wheelchair level. There were forty thousand feet of space in the main area. There was a chapel designed for use by all three major faiths.

By the time our new plant was completed, our working staff numbered over three hundred. We had new orders and new people coming in almost daily.

Our story was known now, our performance record. Some of the jobs we had failed on, in some respects, but we had always corrected the errors. In most cases, however, our products matched or exceeded the quality and time and price levels of the competition.

We were proud of our success in industrial operations, particularly in the field of electronics, printed circuits, wiring of airplane electrical systems, and other mechanisms involved in aircraft production.

It was a steady, going operation and we had a new plant and a whole new vista ahead. This was what we saw; it was what the world, which was beginning to hear about Abilities, saw too.

The Abilities story spread not only in America but around the world. Each week brought visitors from everywhere. It was booming, busy, exciting—an unprecedented industrial and medical adventure.

This was the situation just before that sudden squall

of a recession struck Long Island. We had assumed a great burden. To do so we had gone deeply into debt and the debt had to be serviced and amortized. We did not know at that moment that these new winds were carrying us into danger just ahead—an economic upheaval that would raise the question of whether we would have to close these bright new doors.

## 4

## *A Moment of Truth*

—————————————————————————————————————

In late 1958, a Mid-Western industrialist of vast wealth came to me with an extraordinary idea. "Would you consider taking over the assembling and packaging of a number of our products on a long-range basis?"

It sounded interesting; it involved annually steady productive schedules and nearly a million dollars in gross revenue. We arranged a meeting to discuss the plan.

As the discussion proceeded, I began to realize that we were talking more and more about machines. Doubts began to shadow our words. "You are saying in effect," I told him, "that you would actually automate our plant. You would cut our work staff to a handful of supervisory personnel. Am I correct?"

The Midwesterner nodded. "Primarily, yes. This would be basically a management job, Hank. It would mean phasing out much of the present working force. But of course . . ."

It was a good idea, a practical idea, from his point of view, perhaps from the average business point of view.

From ours, however, it was completely unfeasible. I explained that our first concern had to be our people. If we do not have real jobs for them to do we have lost our first objective—human beings who happened to be disabled but are gainfully and successfully employed, and we have lost, too, the opportunity to do the research on these people at work, to share the new knowledge with others. Spokes and wheels and wires are only a part of the story. There are the people, the staff. And the products they turn out. Our plant without people would be a graveyard.

This was a difficult concept for him to grasp, for we were then, as now, unique in the American business community. Ours has always been a dual role. In the years after we moved to Albertson, we built additional facilities—the building that houses the Human Resources Center, with its laboratories, its training and evaluation facilities, its special pool and gymnasium, its teams of doctors and teachers. But we built it on borrowed funds as we had the first Albertson structure. We had saddled ourselves with debt enough.

As our research programs developed under Human Resources Center, some of these funds for equipment became available and were used. Today, we have full advantage of new federal legislation and the private foundation sources, but this was not so when we began. Ours was an unprecedented venture. The funds had to be honored if we were to begin and to expand. The debt had to be incurred.

I went to those who could be expected to help on this effort we were making—to friends, to foundations, and to the government. Our Center would serve a purpose for the whole community. Other companies and other groups went to these sources; why should we not avail ourselves of whatever legitimate help was there? We had begun as naive, idealistic dreamers, walking into the woods of the industrial world like tenderfoot scouts on their first patrol. We had learned a great deal the hard way. And we were to learn more.

Basically, we set out to rehabilitate people with training, with jobs, and now, in the Human Resources School, with education. There were three phases: education, research and training, and work. All three added up to the final phase of rehabilitation. We took up where the doctors left off.

To us, Abilities Inc. was the priceless clinical laboratory where we could study disabled people at work, and the effects of different training techniques, modification of tools, and machines. It was as important to our final efforts on behalf of the disabled worker as a large hospital was to a medical school. Yet it had to maintain its character and identity to support itself in a competitive environment with disabled workers as its labor force.

It was late in the 1950's when the first real pinch began to be felt. I recall one day one of the first companies for whom we had done subcontracting work in the printed-circuit field was about to send over a new contract for a large order involving more than a hundred thousand dollars. The contract did not arrive. I telephoned to urge them to get it over to us as quickly as possible so we could get started.

"Oh, the lawyers are looking it over," I was told. "It'll be there in a few days."

But it wasn't there. And later phone calls produced the same vague answers. I felt as though I were fighting an invisible antagonist.

Then the word came, a phone call from one of the officials, always one of our good friends. "Hank, I've got a bit of bad news," he said. "That new contract can't go through. It's out for the time being."

No, there was nothing wrong with us, he added, in answer to my query. Our production was fully up to standards and specifications. "The government is cutting back on defense production, for one thing," he told me. "We've lost a number of our major contracts, Hank. We have to think of our own survival."

This translated: whatever work they did have, they would do themselves, simply to keep their machinery rolling, their men on the assembly lines.

Within the next six weeks, there were half-a-dozen similar experiences, contracts and orders on which we had counted failing to come through, projects that had been in the wind dissipating in the suddenly darkening economic skies.

The payroll for Abilities, by then four hundred or more employees, began to loom each week like a grotesque nightmare. Already we were letting a few go. We did not like to do it, but we had no choice.

We had begun this entire complex with a fierce dedication to the problems of disabled people, people who in the starting days nobody wanted to hire. We had said we could find a way, we could solve the problem, we could find paths of productivity for these people.

From the beginning, the workers were our concern in a special way; for most of them this was the first time they had been able to gain real employment, to support their families, to rely on a real job, to earn enough to own a car, buy a small home, raise a family. This was part of our service obligation, without which we had no reason to exist. Others did not have this factor so deeply integrated into their program. Others did not concern themselves about individual physical problems of the people on their staffs, whether they were two-handed or one-handed; they had a physical product to turn out and sell and from which to make a profit. They also had to answer to stockholders or private owners for that profit. The primary dedication was not to the staff because it could not be. It was with us because it had to be.

We had the additional problem of what was to happen to these people who fell before the knife of retreating orders. But we had no choice, we had to let some go; we had to keep Abilities alive, even at the cost of reducing the staff. It was a hard and bitter decision, for we knew these people we had to let go had nowhere else to turn.

That we had done many things wrong, that we had made mistakes, we could not deny. To take risks, to make some mistakes, is business practice; otherwise you are likely to stagnate, atrophy. Our major mistake was that we had started in the most difficult of all areas, the subcontracting field. This is perhaps the poorest type of business on which to build a large organization or one hoping to stay on an even, productive course.

Yet another mistake, from a business point of view, was our insistence that we could build the whole organization from within: every manager and financial man and production-control expert was supposed to come from the bench, regardless of education, experience, background. This meant that our management, which had to compete with the most experienced and sophisticated in industry, had to emerge from our disabled people, most of whom had held no job, or only one or two jobs, before coming to us. All of these were factors in the situation in which we found ourselves in the late 1950's as work began to cancel out, contracts to be cut off, and the workload to drop to a point where twenty-one percent of the staff had to be laid off.

As the *Daily News,* of Thursday, March 13, 1958, reported it:

LAYOFF HITS 65 HANDICAPPED

Abilities, Inc., Albertson employing the physically handicapped, laid off 65 of its 309 employees yesterday as a result of the "general decline of the economy."

The cutback was announced by Henry Viscardi, Jr., president, who said the move was made only after economic pressure made it financially impossible to go with a full staff. The layoffs are effective immediately, Viscardi said.

The cutback was the first in the five-year history of the Long Island firm. All those lopped off the payroll will continue to be covered by health and medical benefit programs.

It was almost 1960 before we realized that we had to begin thinking in totally different terms. We could not gain stability, we could not keep from low periods during which we would have to lay off fifty or a hundred disabled workers, without changing the organization, the whole management procedure.

I would like to point out, however, that we might

have been able to do it in another way—we could have solicited funds to subsidize our workers with "manufactured" work at substandard wages. We could have gone back to the traditional occupations of the handicapped, weaving rugs and making baskets. What we would have lacked would have been human freedom, dignity, opportunity to compete on equal terms. Difficult though it was, we did it the free way, the way we preferred, good or bad, hard or easy. Our disabled people were not only going to earn a fair wage, but they were going to deliver a product on time, meeting the highest production standards. With this came the risks, as they do any business. There were plenty of companies laying off people all around us.

Looking back, there is no question that we were, with all our idealism, actually too ruggedly individualistic, and, I fear, too unrealistic. We didn't seek anybody's help when we began in 1952; we didn't ask anyone to give us a dime, while all around us other firms, some of the biggest and richest in the world, were getting aid. And they were glad to take it too, because government funds helped to purchase plants and machinery to service the government contracts they were fulfilling. We took on the subcontracts to produce parts they needed to complete their contracts. But we were not eligible for this help or subsidies of this kind.

All of this we did on what, looking back today, sounds like a preposterous capitalization. When we needed more, we borrowed; when we had to expand, we borrowed, issuing debentures, obligating ourselves for a debt of more than half a million dollars. As we grew, new contracts required larger material purchases before the parts could be made, shipped and filled. This required funds which we increasingly borrowed from the bank. Our short-range debt grew larger.

This was the situation we had reached when the contracts began to slip away and the need to cut the staff became urgent and the need to find a way out of the diminishing business picture became almost desperate.

It was precisely as we were plunging into the heart of this worsening situation that the President of the United States issued his summons to launch a wholly new program for the mentally retarded. We could hardly face our own problems, much less add a new one.

I remember a night when some of our board met to go over the picture: Art Nierenberg, Joe Landow, Uly Da Parma and Frank Gentile, who was later to direct the Human Resources Center. It was a bleak picture. We had to find some other source of work than exclusively military subcontracting. This was, at that moment, a diminishing economy, especially on Long Island. It was also agreed that our way out was to begin to manufacture products of our own, products we could market on our own, so that we would not be tied exclusively to the large prime contractors.

The question was: What products? And how did we go about maketing them? "What we know about consumer marketing is nil," I pointed out. "We can't just rush in and . . ."

As we talked, we began to explore new avenues, new possibilities. One thing we knew—we would not

give up, or close up. There were a lot of disabled
people to be served.

We had made grim business mistakes and we would
make more. But we would not stand still and be
swamped, either as a work center or a service organization. And that service reached out (or should reach
out, I began to realize), to the mentally retarded
about whom President Kennedy and his sister, Mrs.
Shriver, and all the others on that panel were so concerned.

The situation was curiously confused. On one hand,
we were trying to get back to safe economic ground
with what we had; on the other, we were about to
venture into the absolutely untried, into what could be
the most dangerous kind of quicksand. Where was the
work to support this new group?

This too we discussed. The reaction of most of the
workers was one of uncertainty, but some had already
let it be known: They weren't about to work with any
mentally defective people, any loonies. They had
enough trouble just being crippled.

Sometimes we would have to remind them, "Do you
remember how people reacted to you, before you
came to work here at Abilities?"

You could see in their eyes how, suddenly, they
recalled.

It is easy to look back and see the road strewn with
our errors of commission and omission. But there
are other considerations. Abilities today, as this is
written, is being copied in more than forty-nine other
nations. A whole new venture with which we are co-
operating is being launched in Japan. The number of
workers who have gone forth from Abilities into jobs

in some of the great American corporations, at wages higher than we pay at Abilities, now reaches many, many hundreds. Many of the corporations themselves have employment programs for the handicapped that were started after seeing the Abilities plant and its production experience. Many of their training supervisors, personnel directors, and factory managers have learned about the disabled at our teaching seminars as a result of our research publications.

All of this is true today and was true in those shadowed months at the start of the decade of the sixties. It was a complex two-pronged challenge.

As I review the situation, I think perhaps that a paragraph I found before me on my desk determined my final thinking. It was the opening statement of the President in connection with our meeting in Washington. It seemed to me to articulate the ideas of all of us, and indeed pinpointed the truest meaning of this moment:

The manner in which our nation cares for its citizens and conserves its power resources is more than an index to its concern for the less fortunate. It is a key to the future. Both wisdom and humanity dictate a deep interest in the physically handicapped, the mentally ill, and the mentally retarded. Yet, although we have made considerable progress in the treatment of physical handicaps, although we have attacked on a broad front the problems of mental illness, although we have made great strides in the battle against disease, we as a nation have for too long postponed an intensive search for solutions to the problem of the mentally retarded. That failure should be corrected.

PART TWO:

*TRIALS AND ERRORS*

## 5

## *Battle to Survive*

In the fall of 1961, Abilities was only in the probing stage in the matter of an employment program for the mentally retarded. The President had asked us to do something, and left the manner and nature of it to us. Eunice Shriver had seen our plant and had told us to go full speed ahead; so also had her husband at our Baltimore meeting. The retreat of our sales and contracts continued; the need for the military hardware we had been working on was lessening. The Long Island area, geared primarily to military production in electronics, was hard hit. Small companies were going under. Layoffs were widespread. Diversification was the answer, we all knew. But I was not about to compound our problems by laying off physically disabled workers and replacing them with mentally retarded workers.

We could try for a federal grant, however, Sargent Shriver had assured me, if we could come up with any kind of program acceptable to the office of Vocational Rehabilitation of the Health, Education and Welfare Department.

Mary Switzer had already supported many of our Research studies in Telemetry and Bioengineering. A possible answer loomed, an unknown, perhaps perilous, idea: to begin a product diversification program within Abilities itself, with the training and employment of the mentally retarded, one that would be divorced from the manufacture of military electronic components.

It was a singularly ironic idea, I thought, as I explored it in my own mind; the possibility that the mentally retarded, instead of being one more burden we had to assume, might provide a partial solution to our own problem. It was not simply that we would get money for training and research. It could mean a start at finding a product, a new avenue of services not tied to subcontracting or military necessity.

I talked it over with Art, Frank Gentile, and Joe Landow, with some of the foremen and department heads. Reactions were mixed, often dubious. The first, which Art delineated sharply, was that we did not know whether we could succeed in making these people perform properly in any work program we devised. With the physically disabled it had been a physical problem, an engineering challenge. With the mentally retarded, it was nothing you could see or touch, often nothing you could recognize or understand. As a classified disability, mental retardation has existed almost exclusively as an educational measurement. As much as three percent of the adult population is to some degree retarded, although generally unrecognized and unclassified as such.

Moreover, I began to get the first sparks from the foremen and others about bringing in mentally retarded workers. An instinctive prejudice was there, a fact that could not be hidden. We had seen it from the start and we knew we would have to deal with it if any plan actually went into effect. One foreman told me bluntly, "I don't like it. Men with no arms or legs I can work with and train, but how do I train a dummy?"

There it was—reaction that we would have to face. And the people on our own Board, when I called them into a special meeting to discuss the whole picture, also had deep and, in some instances almost implacable, misgivings. "Look, you're taking on something you know nothing about," one board member pointed out. "How do you know it may not be too big for you?"

How did I know? The answer, blunt and harshly put, was, I didn't.

Yet I knew we somehow had to make it work. We had to begin to think in terms of evaluation and training problems, development of teaching techniques. Earlier I had talked with Arthur Roth at the Franklin National Bank about a possible beginning of diversification in handling some phases of data processing or related areas of service for the bank. Roth, who is most imaginative and had been a supporter from the start, suggested school savings or mortgage loan services.

To deal with the economic problems we were facing, a small group of our top people began to meet in early-morning and sometimes after-hours sessions in my office to discuss production, cutbacks, and economies that we could initiate. On the question of the MR's, we split into two groups—one to consider their possible use in electronical operations; the other to consider their potential in clerical operations for the bank. I had again discussed the idea with Roth. If it were feasible at all to use them, it would involve considerable experimentation in training techniques. We were all highly dubious; most of us had never knowingly seen a mentally retarded worker up to this time. Roth was encouraging and enthusiastic.

At Abilities in those days there was tremendous activity going on to weather the storm, to rechart and reset our course. Art was busy trying to replace some of our top management who had had to be let go in our efforts to tighten up organization and get maximum results. He was also trying to find new salesmen to bolster our sales department and bring in new business. Accounts payable were stretched way out. Receivables were equally bad for everyone was in trouble. Cash flow was a day-to-day battle. To meet payrolls became a problem. In addition to the payroll, the short-term debt owed to the bank was a constant threat as payments were deferred.

There were several battles raging at once, on several fronts—all within the seemingly serene (on the surface) triumphant operation we had under way. How could we fail; our cause was too noble. It was Camelot all over again.

For instance, there was a time when things were so tight we actually could not pay our phone bill, which runs, of course, into thousands of dollars monthly. The phone company was quietly, but insistently, letting me know that they were just about to turn us off. I checked with some top people and got word back that I shouldn't worry too much. "Look," they said, "they won't cut off the service. We shouldn't tell you this,

but they won't. When the chips are down, they won't
shut it off. They'll make it tough for you, curtail the
service, but they'll never close you down."

Art didn't believe it. He suggested we use homing
pigeons. But the phone company just couldn't face
doing it, I learned. Still, they sure made it rough on us
for a few months, telephonically speaking.

Following our discussions with Arthur Roth, we
began to outline a program of training concepts. We
would bring in specialists—psychologists and sociologists trained in interpersonal relations and evaluations
—to launch a personnel-evaluation program for the
mentally retarded. To find suitable work force, many
would have to be screened. We would bring in specialists who were already working with MR's who knew
their problems, their mental and emotional abilities
and disabilities. We talked to people within our own
area who worked in these fields, psychiatrists and
physicians. They agreed with our idea of beginning
with mentally retarded teenagers, boys and girls who
were not yet too frustrated and twisted by defeat and
rejection in their attempts to compete on normal
terms, under standard everyday conditions in the
normal world. These would be educable retarded, who
if they could be trained, had a potential for work. We
would evaluate them and train them to take their
places on specific jobs—if we could get the jobs. Arthur Roth was willing to give us a chance to develop
some banking programs at the Franklin National. He
continued to look with favor on their school savings
program. It involved quite a staff and handled about
four million dollars. The problem of financing the
evaluation and training was ours, and, as I saw it, to

be shared with the government, or with private foundations, if we could obtain such aid.

Armed with plans, ideas, and at least one possibility for a bona-fide job involving MR's, we went to Washington to talk with Commissioner Mary Switzer and her staff at the Office of Vocational Rehabilitation. This meeting was held at the suggestion of Sargent and Eunice Shriver, both of whom were present, as well as members of Vocational Rehabilitation's research staff, including old friends such as J. Russell Dean, Dr. James Garett, and Dr. William Usdane. At this meeting we were to present at least preliminary plans of a program.

Shriver had asked us to come down with some kind of program that could be used as a jumping-off point. Now he wanted to know—with his usual direct approach—what did we have in mind?

As succinctly and directly as I could, I began to describe our concept of an evaluation and training program with an ultimate objective of enabling the MR's to do clerical banking assignments and electronic assembly jobs. In regard to the latter, I pointed out that whatever electronics work we had on hand was being adequately taken care of by our already reduced working staff. Involving the MR's in electronics was still in the planning and development stage, indeed not even that far advanced. New training techniques using work simplification, work factors and audio-visual training aids had to be developed. I informed Shriver candidly, "For us to get a grant to provide a demonstration training program is almost meaningless unless we can also get work. We can't train new people to take other people's jobs in our own plant. We've got to have a new work load or the whole idea has to be scrapped. The experiment must be controlled, so that to place them elsewhere at the outset just won't work."

I have always believed in the principle of being as realistic and open as possible in such situations. The better they knew exactly where we stood and why, the less chance there was of any kind of misconception.

Shriver understood the point. "It's no problem, Hank," he assured me. Then, abruptly returning to the first step, he said, "Now, let's talk about some support." Mary Switzer in her patient, thoughtful manner explained that what I was describing was a demonstration research project to find new ways of training the mentally retarded. It sounded exciting. She was encouraging.

"And what would be the cost—your needs, Hank?"

While I had no idea, we had handled some research demonstration projects before this. I was among old friends. I practically drew a figure out of the Washingtonian air. "For equipment, personnel, manpower, and general operating costs," I answered, "I would say fifty to a hundred thousand dollars for the first year."

I had no detailed budget at that time, no set procedures, no protocol for handling the grant; however, the figure was one that did closely approximate the overall needs.

I knew it would be months before any program could go into full-scale action, and by then Abilities' financial picture could be changed. I wasn't going to paint the blackest picture I could of the momentary situation. What I told Shriver was: "Look, Abilities is

in trouble. I am not going to lay off disabled people
and hire these retarded folks, even if we're correct in
that these people can be trained and employed. If I'm
going to set up this demonstration, I need work in my
shop to do it, and the only people who can give me
that work are people in industry, and Long Island
right at this instant is practically a disaster area."

Getting in work has always been the heart of Abilities' battle for survival. Although at present it was
grimmer than ever before, it was still the same situation as when we started. The main difference was one
of degree—our payroll and inventory. Now we had to
keep on hand tens of thousands of dollars worth of
inventory and our weekly payroll was running over
forty-five thousand dollars. Meanwhile, with no re-
serve, our cash flow position was precarious. Accounts
payable and receivable were adjusted from day to day.
We owed people. Others owed us. Debentures were
due to be redeemed at year end. The mortgage payments were due monthly. The payments on the short-
term bank loans were now accumulating in dangerous
default.

There was also the possible problem of space. If all
the possibilities clicked, in spite of present layoffs,
there was the possibility that we would need more
space to house the increase in personnel because of the
retarded. There were, at that time, no federal funds
for such construction. Our only hope lay in either a
private foundation grant for construction or in renting
the space needed.

I decided not to raise the question. If all went well it
would be delightful to face this problem if and when it
arose.

All through the years we had insisted on going it

alone. Let our customers get big contracts. Let other companies get their tools from government procurement designed to aid military subcontractors, small and large. We had stayed clear of all such things. As a workshop for the disabled, we were not eligible. We had stuck it out on our own.

We had received assistance from our friends in VRA through our research and demonstration grants, but never in running the shop. This time, though, it had to be different. The President wanted us in the field of retardation, and we were anxious and ready to help. But, I thought, this time we had well better get some aid for our program because our situation was critical without the added burden.

I thought a moment about our relationship with our good friend Arthur Roth and Franklin National. I thought to myself: "He has been our friend. If anybody puts pressure on Roth, he would have the right to be offended." Sargent Shriver said, "Isn't there one company on Long Island where we might help?"

This was the same thing. If they put pressure, if only a letter, on any of our friends, it could wreck any possible new jobs. So I said, "Well, I just can't think of any at the moment."

Shriver looked at me with a smile, and the meeting with the VRA people ended successfully. They agreed to present our grant request to their council if we would draw up data and figures. At a subsequent meeting, Jim Garrett and his staff were most kind in suggesting a suitable design for the project request. They really liked the idea as unique and different.

As the meeting ended, Shriver came over to me and put his arm around my shoulders.

"Look," he said, "why don't you be a good fellow?

Name me just one company that you want to go after."

I appreciated what he was trying to do. He wanted to bring us into closer contact with people and companies who would help with an important project. But I felt that any interference would antagonize our good customers and we could not afford that. The only company I could think of where we couldn't get hurt was International Business Machines. We had been trying to get IBM business for five years, without managing even a ripple on the water. So I mentioned International Business Machines. I also mentioned MacDonald Aircraft of St. Louis. MacDonald had just been awarded a long-term government contract. Republic Aircraft, which formerly had had a large volume of business available for subcontract to us, had lost out on the bidding. They were in bad shape as a result and were laying off thousands of workers. We knew MacDonald would have plenty of business on hand for a long time to come.

IBM is a great company which believes in the disabled. We bid like any others trying to get subcontract work. For five years we had been knocking at their doors. One of their people told one of our representatives on an early visit to their offices, "You have asked to be no different from any other supplier. We have one man who spent seven years trying to become a supplier to our company. However, he has since supplied us for many years."

The fact that we went in on artificial limbs and in wheelchairs—I am proud to report—never got us any business per se. We wanted meaningful work that would be profitable to use and needed by our cus-

tomer. We did not trade on sympathy. We were not
industrial mendicants seeking a crust of old steel to
salvage. We sold marketable skills at a price like any
one else. It was the way we had wanted it from the
start; it was the way things remained.

It wasn't until we were standing in the corridor outside the VRA office waiting for the elevator that I
mentioned the names of these two firms to Shriver.

"I think either one of them could help us; they've
both got plenty of work. And I know we could help
them. We could do the kind of job they need, we've
shown that we can do the job."

I figured that would be the end of it. We had the
promise of consideration for our grant for the training
program, and this meant that the clerical banking
program was that much closer to reality. The Franklin
National Bank people were with us.

We would begin on a very small scale, using bank
personnel at the start and slowly working in the disabled and the MR's as they were trained. Funds would
be available to support the evaluation and training
phases of the program. We now had a chance to start.
At least we had made the first step.

The wheels turned slowly. The meeting in Washington was in the late fall of 1961. By December, Roth
had agreed to let us move one of the banking operations into our own plant. He was enthusiastic about
the idea and confident of its success. I had promised
that once the disabled and later, the retarded, were
trained, we would do the work as efficiently as, and at
a savings to, the bank. We had been talking with Vice
President John Sadlik and the Franklin National people for almost a year about the possibility of participat-

ing in their Junior Banking program—a school savings program the bank had developed on Long Island
in which children in each class make regular savings
on a weekly basis. The program was designed to develop saving habits and an understanding of banking
processes by actual participation. The children wrote
out deposit slips and the funds were gathered by class
tellers and ultimately taken to the bank by messenger
where the processing of these junior accounts took
place. Originally, the idea had been that we would
participate only to the extent of sending some of our
employees to the bank to take on part-time processing
assignments. These workers were to be physically disabled, not mentally retarded, employees. I felt Abilities itself had no real role in such a plan; we delivered
the people, they did the work somewhere else. How
much more meaningful it would be if we could take
over the entire banking operation.

In our first discussions, Roth had suggested we try
some of the operations used in the stock register and
transfer departments. Junior Banking was, in fact, a
secondary idea. But as our business worsened, we
decided to go along with the Junior Banking program,
hoping to be able to bring in the mentally retarded on
the assignment, whether or not we ever got the research and demonstration grant from Washington. We
needed work even if we had to send our people out of
our shop and over to the bank. Arthur Roth and the
Franklin people were aware of this and wanted to help
our diversification plans. They believed in the possibilities of the retarded and were willing to go along.
After countless conferences, we agreed that as a start,
regardless of what final course we followed, we would

take a long hard look at the Junior Banking program and see if we felt we could come up with techniques and procedures for training our physically disabled staff to do the job better than the bank itself, and at a savings in cost to the bank.

Junior Banking was set up in one of Franklin's main buildings on the Island. We spent a long time watching it; we had our people examine each step in the processing, asking questions of the operators themselves.

Seeing it from this close-up vantage point, we became very enthusiastic about it. We could do this kind of job effectively, and it would mark the start of a diversification program that would keep us from the kind of economic squeeze in which we found ourselves at that moment. It was a big program, run as a service by Franklin National. It involved 129 elementary schools, nearly 80,000 accounts that had to be processed regularly, and some $3,500,000 of funds in the total average balance on hand. The cash deposits would be handled by us and posted with the banking machines just as at a teller's window.

Of course, our venture into banking, even though we began, not with MR's, but with our physically disabled staff, was an issue of discussion and debate within our own shop. The manufacturing executives and foremen could not see the wisdom of moving from manufacturing and electronics activities, which we had been in from the start, to the banking business, about which none of us knew a thing. Some of our top people told me frankly that they thought we would get deeper into trouble rather than out of it by such a move.

But we had to take some step and it was my decision to move ahead on the banking operation after
Franklin National Bank agreed to let us try. They did
more than that. From Roth, the boss man, on down,
their people had agreed to back us, to train our people, to help us in the start of this new venture. Then, as
and when the grant came through, we would begin to
work with the mentally retarded and phase them into
the banking and electronic assembly jobs, returning
the physically disabled to new business we hoped to be
bringing into the shop. There were a lot of 'ifs.' This
was the plan of action—along with the further plan of
moving the Junior Savings, once we took it over, into
our own plant. By the spring of 1962, the grant for
research in training mentally retarded workers had
been approved. By Easter, we were ready to transfer
the banking operation, which some of our workers had
carefully studied at bank headquarters, to Abilities
itself.

This raised additional problems. The processing of
these accounts was a long-established operation run by
a staff at one of the bank's main centers. Shortly after
Easter we planned the active transfer of the furniture
and equipment and banking machines from Franklin
National to Abilities.

It was a complex situation we faced, a tortuous
route by which we hoped to bring in our first major
diversification. We would transfer the entire personnel
of Franklin's Junior Savings Department to Abilities,
and they would continue the operation until all the
non-disabled had been gradually replaced by our own
employees. This would include the supervisors. How it
would work out none of us knew. How would these

people feel about working in a plant alongside the disabled? Not to mention our ultimate objective: the mentally retarded whom we intended to bring in and train as quickly as we could. All of the bank's employees were guaranteed jobs back at the main branches as they were replaced by our people. This helped in their attitude.

It was still going to be a shock to these women, as it would be to any group of normal male or female workers, to find themselves moved from the routines and personnel to which they were accustomed and set down in a plant of a totally different kind, among workers missing limbs, arms and hands.

I talked to some of the ladies, brought some of those who had been in charge of the operation for years out to the plant, where we had a delightful lunch and toured Abilities and met the workers. Two groups came out for these luncheons, on two different occasions. They saw not only Abilities but Human Resources Center and our school. It was obvious that they were impressed and somewhat relieved. I could see in reality what we had been trying to tell them—that we were really happy people, there wasn't any blood around. It wasn't depressing. Rather, it was exhilarating because we were all enthusiastic about achieving our goal. Their reaction was warm and friendly, and I was able to go back to Franklin's vice-president, John Sadlik, and tell him I thought it was going to be all right. However, I had to be assured—as I was—that they would stand behind us. The venture couldn't be just a tryout from which we could all run if things didn't go smoothly at the start.

"It can't be just a picnic if the sun shines," I told

Sadlik. "This is a picnic—rain, ants, snow, no matter what. We're going through with this."

In a friendly, patient manner he reminded me that banking in general was no picnic. And on that the vice-president and I, neither of us having the least idea what the weather would be, firmly shook hands.

6

*Minds and Machines*

Over the Easter holidays, in April, 1962, we moved
the whole Junior Savings banking operation into our
plant—desks and chairs, the posting machine, coin-
sorting machines, wastebaskets and files and coat-
rack. Since the schools were closed and no classroom
deposits were coming in, this was an opportune time
for the move. On Monday morning—April 23, 1962
—the entire crew from the bank came in. All of
them were women, regular bank employees and only a
few of our disabled, who had been assigned at the
bank. So there was the first team from the bank and
there was the physical setup in our plant, waiting for
them to sit down and start to work. Surrounded by
us.

No MR's had been brought in. The grant had been
approved in March, but funds were not yet available.
Only when they were in hand could the training programs be launched. What was happening was that two
diverse operations, which would in due course merge,
were being launched almost simultaneously: the bank

processing operation and the evaluation training and
work programs of the MR's. A charming lady who had
been in charge of Junior Savings at the bank remained
in this post when the operation moved to our plant,
but her position was a nominal one. We designated
one of our disabled people—a cardiac—as pro tem
manager, a first step in the takeover by our personnel.

When we began to discuss seriously with this
woman and her co-workers our idea of eventually having the MR's take over, she and her staff were somewhat disturbed. Although they knew that in due
course they were scheduled to be transferred from
Junior Banking to other positions back at the bank
itself, the idea of being replaced by mentally retarded
people upset some of them both personally and profes-
sionally. I can't say that I blame them; bankers after
all do come in for enough abuse.

Several admitted this quite frankly. Their work
calculations—whether done by hand, mechanically, or
electronically—had to be accurate. They did not comprehend how the retarded could be trained for such jobs.
One of them told an Abilities supervisor: "This entire
thing is folly. It won't work out, whether you use the
physically disabled or these others you are talking about.
The Junior Savings is going to wind up back at the
bank, where I think it belongs anyway."

Of course, we did work in the disabled, gradually,
because it was part of the plan, and some of the bank
people on the job began to see how effective these
disabled were at their tasks. Actually, many of these
workers we brought in had performed far more complicated jobs in our industrial operations; for them, the

clerical banking assignments were less demanding.

During the spring of 1962, training procedures were developed, and in the fall of that year we began to screen and train young retardees, male and female, for jobs in both the industrial operation and the banking program. Most of the techniques were evolved by our own people, the physically handicapped, working with outside experts in emotional and psychological problems of the sort we would face in the evaluation training and employment of MR's in our plant operations.

But the underlying feeling of uncertainty, resentment, and concern about this program did not go away easily. Our foreman, who had forgotten that he himself was in a wheechair, was reported to have said: "It's bad enough trying to teach guys with no arms or legs to do the jobs we do here. Now we have to start on people who got soft heads. How are we going to teach them to do a coil-winding operation?"

Somehow we did.

I think of some of the people who have come to us. Outstanding among them is the almost incredible development in the talents of a Negro girl whom no one wanted to hire. She became a leader in the coil-winding operation, an intricate machine that winds copper coil many hundreds of times around spools used in computer complexes and other mechanisms. Although the operation is mostly mechanical, a series of repetitive actions must be performed: first, the spools must be set in place and then the wound coils must be removed. This girl, after a period of indoctrination and training, wound a thousand spools a day, about six hundred more than anyone else. The job was her life, and she delighted in it. The average person sitting down before those winding machines six or eight hours a day, five days a week, performing the same ceaseless whirling routine, would wind up talking to himself. But as the people on the floor have it, "she talks to the machines, and they answer back."

Some who knew of our goal to train these children-people—for they seemed like children even though many were in their early twenties—asked if we were not picking exactly the wrong moment to start in on something as new and different as this. My answer was a question in turn: "What time is the right time? Was there a 'right time' to start Abilities in the first place?"

The truth is that any time is the right time, or the wrong time, depending on the point of view. Any time is the right time for a new and original idea. Any time is the right time for something we believe is important. Of course, it was a crazy notion, looked at from the normal routines of business. The reaction of average businessmen to our approach is predictable and, from their point of view, correct. Particularly if I were to tell them that we were about to take on mentally retarded workers who had never before been able to work at anything above sedentary sweeping and similar jobs; that we were going to train them to do clerical operations and reasonably detailed banking and machine operations on an electronic assembly line; and what is more, that after we shook the knots out of these jobs, we'll make a profit from them. To take on a task like that, one must believe deeply with both heart and mind. That is why I thank God for people like Arthur Roth and his associates at the Franklin National Bank.

So the MR's came in. They came from the school districts and through various agencies and groups formed by parents of the mentally retarded. They came in for evaluation and testing, then for the beginning of the training program. It was a curious confrontation—they and us. In the months that we had been working on this new development, work from several major sources had been assured, through our own efforts and with some assists from Washington, especially from the Shrivers. The talks with Sargent Shriver were to pay off. These projects meant the possibility of being able to hold our disabled workers and at the same time provide for the adolescent trainees we were bringing in.

Assessing the situation in the fall of 1962, I could state: we had projects lined up, training programs set up and ready to start, and the banking project rolling smoothly. Our disabled were replacing the bank's people and the MR's were about to be trained to replace them.

Training was still in the formative stage. There was no experience in this field to draw on; we had to wait to see what actions and reactions took place. We had brought in as part of the training staff two young women, Chana Schachner and Ruth Kass, experts respectively, in cultural education and education in special situations. Both reported that it was very difficult to find information on this kind of MR training; there were no practical programs to observe, nothing in the libraries, next to nothing in journals and reports. It was a field virtually devoid of reference material or records of achievement.

We had never before had a clerical training program at Abilities. We did, however, have an industrial training program on which we could start the MR's. Here we developed audio-visual techniques—slides showing an object, material, machines, what we wanted, what the worker did, one step at a time, visually displayed on the screen, with the units themselves at hand for the trainee to see and feel and operate. Now we added a clerical training program, beginning in a small way by teaching girls to handle money, to count, add and subtract, and perform other simple operations. Always we sought to train by detailed job methodization and work simplification. Break the job down into logical simplification steps with limited concentration and lots of repetition. By this method we hoped to be able to arrive at some evaluations.

Describing her own experience when she saw these new workers for the first time, Ruth Kass told me, "They were charming, but they were like children, real children. You wouldn't have guessed that many were older than sixteen, that many were actually over twenty-one, although the majority were adolescents. But I didn't see them or look at them as MR's. The terminology didn't mean anything to me and I didn't want it to. I saw them as perfectly lovely, well-behaved, generally socially adjusted youngsters. No one seeing them on the street would have picked them out as being mentally retarded."

We started bringing in machines on which they would learn—typewriters, adding machines, billing machines. Much of what they had to learn was simple routine: setting down figures, punching keys, pulling levers, taking a paper out, putting another paper in, taking off a row of figures, and so on—all actions that could be performed as a routine, one step at a time.

Behind the research training program, even then, was the germ of an exciting new potential: we would be pushing their abilities, goals, and achievements beyond levels they had ever before attempted. Several years later, one of the top educators working with us, a man with a special background in the field of MR's, Dr. Leonard S. Blackman, was to sum up this philosophy: "People ask me why we teach history to the retarded—they have such a poor time perspective. Or why geography—they are so immobile, where will they go that geography will be important to them? Or speech therapy—what do they have to say that is so important, anyway? The point is, if you do these things, you find that the person can make progress and function at a higher level than he was able to do before. I think that is really all you have to do to justify this approach. What this project is doing is saying there is no predicted limit, let us push them to whatever their limit may be but we do not know what that is."

At the start, we knew even less. We felt our way. We would start them in filing, then posting. We would teach them by example, by audio-visual training, by special personal instruction, above all, by simplifying each operation and by repetition, over and over and over, until they were able to assess themselves, catch their own mistakes. They were slow, yes; difficult, yes; but they were eager, they wanted to learn. This was a great and incredible fact—their eagerness to learn. We were opening up to them—in what seemed to us drab, routine, machine-like operations—a new world, a magnificent, exciting world, a world of learners, producers, people.

They would come to filing. At first, this was difficult for us, and them. Filing requires putting ideas together: this must go with that, this belongs before that or after that. Where it goes isn't something tangible. They have to think about it.

As Chana describes this part of the training, "It is a judgment on their part more than anything else. They have to make an evaluation and the situation changes with each card, each item they have to file. Where does this go? What do I do with this one? They have to start learning the process letter by letter matching it, thinking of its place in the alphabet. It may seem simple to us, but for them it is a difficult concept and a learning process."

Fortunately, we had a small group and we were able to have our young teachers work with them closely. They reacted best in the one-to-one training relationship, rather than in the group situation. In filing, it was almost all an individual person-to-person approach.

But it was working. This was the one significant fact we discovered: it worked from the start. These adolescent MR's, who in most cases had been written off as unemployable for skilled tasks, were learning practical skills and operations. Aside from their own eagerness, they now had two things going for them: our research into new concepts of a training program at Abilities, and the special classes in the public high schools (designed specifically for these children-adults), which had been set up under the Vocational Rehabilitation Administration program sponsored by the federal government, the first such experiment ever attempted on Long Island. This, too, had been worked out in consultations with Mary Switzer's staff in Washington, and with Bill Spinelli of our local Division of Vocational Rehabilitation. The MR's spent half a day with us (three-and-a-half hours) and the other half in special classes at the public high schools. At the completion of their high-school course, they would be entitled to a certificate testifying to their vocational training and aptitudes.

These young people ranged from seventeen to twenty, most of them girls. They came into the operation unsure and somewhat frightened, but they were quiet, reserved. The girls were clean and neat, but often made no effort to make themselves attractive; they frequently wore little makeup, their clothes were somewhat dowdy, uncolorful. Much of this was to change in future weeks and months, as the story of the MR's and their role at Abilities unfolded.

In September, with the opening of public schools, the Junior Banking program moved into full operation. At this time, our people began to take over the whole operation. I brought in one of our top management team, Marion Watson, polio-paralyzed and in a wheelchair, a charming lady and long-time friend as well as one of our most level-headed executives. Although she was thoroughly familiar with the handling of clerical and accounting activities, Marion had been given a crash-course in Junior Banking over the summer. In September she was placed in charge of the program although she worked closely with those of the bank's staff who remained. At the same time we brought in four more of our physically disabled. The MR's were not yet involved.

Audio-visual training with the retarded proved an

effective technique. Through film and voice training we knew we could make cable-makers and plug-solderers and coil-winders out of them. But clerical work would take longer. We soon learned the audio-visual methods would not apply. For testing and training we used a checkout-counter procedure, just as one finds in a supermarket. The trainees "play store" with groceries. They learn the keyboard of the cash register, learn to handle money, to count change, accomplishments important to the actual banking operation.

Early in the fall this training program released Joanne and Elizabeth and the two girls were sent to join Marion Watson in the banking operation. Some of the bank workers, hearing that the two mentally retarded girls were being brought in, reiterated their conviction that MR's couldn't learn to post records on the machines accurately. "I hope it will work for you —but I wonder if it can," one girl from the bank told Marion. But the well-mannered young women came in and sat down at their machines ready to begin work. Their performance was excellent for their first day and steadily improved. Other mentally retarded girls were brought in. An industrial revolution of a new sort was beginning. Marion was in full charge, on my specific orders.

There was opposition to the idea not only within the banking group, but also in the plant. There were all sorts of rumors, stories, murmurs of trouble. I had some misgivings myself. Were the girls and boys we were bringing in, the retarded, going to work out? What about our efficiency rating? There were reports of serious mistakes. And then came a jolting episode —two of the MR's we had brought into Junior Banking got into a fight. One girl put a cover from one of the machines over the head of another girl and began punching her. Marion, returning from lunch, heard their screams as she approached the office and stepped into the situation at once. She succeeded in separating them, thus ending the battle. Then she sent word to the training supervisor, as she had been instructed to do in the event of any disorder or other problem. The supervisor came in quickly and calmed the staff. Then she took the two girls aside and explained quietly that this was not ladylike, it was not adult, it was not the way adult workers behaved.

Simple, yes. But with the children-women it was extraordinarily successful. They were aware of their mistake; they were struggling, as we all were, not to lose what they had here. Shocking as such a contretemps might seem in terms of office law, Marion and I discussed it in quite different terms. To maintain her production level, Marion already had her problems and, of course, such a situation as had just occurred added to them. But it did not matter, she said. I recall I remember asking her, "Well, Marion, are you disillusioned? Do you feel life is complicated enough without having to take on a group like this?"

"No," she answered quickly. "No, they aren't that bad. Because one thing happens doesn't mean we have to wash out the whole plan."

I said, "Come on, Marion. We've worked together for years."

"I'm not trying to be a hero, Mr. Viscardi," she said. "I know it's a challenge. I know I can make it."

"No doubt about it? None at all?"

I had to be sure of her feelings, sure that she understood that this was not one isolated instance, that she was willing to cope with the many new problems which would arise. I asked her if she didn't agree that this kind of office brawl was anything but normal behavior.

"It's not normal, of course," she answered. "But it will work out; it has to work out."

I wondered. We were dealing with people strange to us, and we were dealing with the lives of these people. We were also treading on untrod industrial ground. We were obligating ourselves to deliver products: on the one hand, a banking service for school accounts; on the other, industrial and electronic products and assemblies. Not only the future of these people, but of Abilities was at stake. It was no excuse to our customers that we were engaged in a noble experiment.

There was to be a sequel to that minor lunch-hour slugfest. It took place a few weeks later—the same office, the same two girls, the same situation.

Marion, gentle and understanding as she is, can imbue that understanding with a steely realism. When the second fight occurred, I received the report from the supervisor and a brief message from Marion: Joanne had been suspended for three days for breach of ladylike conduct in the office.

Marion imposed the suspension. That simple act of ordinary discipline was the end of trouble with Joanne. Marion had made the girl realize that the office was no place for tantrums.

There were no more office fights, arguments, tantrums. To Marion, her success with Joanne was her first important victory, because Joanne was a star in the actual banking procedures. She was exceptionally accurate. "In some ways," Marion told me, "she knows more about the program than I do. Some of the things she knows—her scope of understanding of this banking setup—are unbelievable."

What kind of girl was she? A beautiful girl who came from a good family and was unaware that there was anything wrong with her. She was well-dressed, she was poised, she was very attractive. If you saw her picture on a magazine cover, you would have thought she was a model. Watching her at her work, you would hardly have guessed that there was the slightest thing wrong. This became more and more true as time went on, as she became more adjusted.

And so with all the MR's. As they continued to work, changes took place in all of them. That phenomenon caused considerable comment; also it helped to calm the storms of opposition we encountered from both staff and workers. The MR's were like children, they looked like children when they first came in— young teen-aged girls in bobby-socks. Then slowly they began to change.

They were working now, earning money; they bought clothes for themselves, they became aware of makeup. I guess they went home and told their mothers, "I want to wear lipstick. Why can't I wear lipstick like other girls?"

And the mothers would say, "Yes, why not?"

And they had their hair set, and some, among them Elizabeth who had had the fight with Joanne, began going every week to the beauty parlor.

In this project there were, of course, both men and

women. There were other minor disturbances, sometimes violence. They didn't all work out, for one reason or another. But the MR's who really developed, as many as thirty to forty percent left us because they had learned new skills and were able to go out into the world, to get other jobs. Many have stayed with us. Our experimental research continues beyond Junior Savings.

One boy and girl, cousins, were in their late teens or early twenties. The boy was often in trouble; he liked to boast of his friends in juvenile gangs, of the "rumbles" he had been part of. At Abilities he learned machine work and then he left us and got an even better job. There were occasional difficulties, but he was doing good work. The girl stayed with us. And the youth wanted it that way. "Don't let her go to some other plant," he pleaded with our people. "She belongs with you."

It was an interesting twist. If he couldn't always take care of himself, he at least had deep concern for her and he would call us from time to time to make sure that she was safe.

What we began to find out—all of us, from top management to the newest non-MR worker—was that the MR girls and boys were simply other human beings, with a disability different from ours, but with abilities that could be developed and, as they were developed, the individuals grew too, became more controlled, tractable, able to live more nearly normal lives. The MR's on the other hand felt a deep concern for our disabled workers and did many little things to aid them.

The clearest example of that can be seen in the recording of a typical verbal report by one of our training supervisors on a young MR girl.

I'd like to speak of Elaine. The overall impression we first had of Elaine was, we have to keep our eye on her; she's attractive, that's obvious, and she was boy crazy. That was the only way to describe her when she came in. But don't forget that these youngsters have had a lot of failures in school, and with their families too. Some come in as failures. They've failed so many times that they've accepted the fact that this is what is expected of them. We've had them express this to us. They say, "Oh, after all, I'm in a special class."

Elaine had this attitude. When she sat down at the typewriter and couldn't handle it, it was just another failure and she reacted accordingly. When we found something that she could do, and we encouraged her to do it, she became interested and excited about it. This other problem, the emphasis on boys, lessened a great deal.

But you see she's been able to adjust to a large extent, to comprehend a certain series of values and relate to them. If you walk into the cafeteria now when Elaine is at lunch, you can be sure she'll be flirting. I'm sure she's involved with the boys; I'm sure she dates. However, she has reached the point (and it is a great thing for her), where she knows that from a certain specified time to another specified time, *when I work, this is my obligation. My obligation is to perform my banking duties, not to flirt, not to goof off,* as she calls it herself. To that extent she has matured. I think that Elaine can be married. I think she can be a mother. She may not be the best wife and mother, but she won't be the worst. And she's the girl who is generally capable of managing.

Step by step the retarded people took over a great share of Junior Banking. Of course, when errors occurred anywhere in the operation, some people seemed to take special delight in insisting that it was because the staff handling the posting were MR's. But the truth was, as month followed month, their record began to shape up to an accuracy higher than that of the non-retarded staff which had been performing the same tasks.

As one training foreman put it: "Yes, they are different, they are sometimes like children. But they can be taught. They learn to do that part of the job for which they are responsible. And an interesting feature of this is that most of them stay with it; they like the feeling that they are producing. This is their triumph. You get more time and more effort out of these workers because they want to stay on the bench; they don't have to get up so often and take a walk or get a cup of coffee or seek some other diversion. In some ways, in many cases, what they do is extraordinary."

We at Abilities are not going to solve all the problems, of course. What we set out to do was to establish a new profitable operation and at the same time to prove that we could make productive citizens of the mentally retarded. They didn't have to spend their lives raking lawns.

What we had done by starting the MR program was to bring the retarded into a new relationship with life

—a working, productive relationship, an earning relationship. While doing this we were experimenting in whole new areas of education and training techniques which would be of benefit to all industry and to the retarded. Now they were people who could go out and buy their own things.

All of this happened and is happening as I set these facts down. It continues to be a challenge to us, because our business is not work alone, but, as I have stated earlier, people, and a very special kind of people. This is a fact we cannot forget or overlook. As long as these special people have parents or families or other relatives to watch out for them, they have no serious problems; all we have done is to add a new meaning and richness to their lives. But what happens to those whose parents are dead; whose family is gone or scattered, whose relatives are unable to cope with, or are indifferent to, their problems? Where are they to go? Who will watch out for them?

Because these people are a part of the overall operation of Abilities, we are already thinking of these questions. Perhaps some kind of half-way home will be the answer.

For now we know, at least, that the MR people have worked out at Abilities. One step on the road to diversification for us, and stability for them, had been taken. The question of our stability as an enterprise, with its own products and markets, remained to be solved.

Like so many of our people, we too, as Abilities, were a special case.

# 7

## *A Man Named Hans*

At Albertson, three forces were together as a unit: a work center called Abilities, a research laboratory we call the Human Resources Research & Training Institute, and a school for the physically disabled child who otherwise has no chance to get an education—the Human Resources School. Each is a separate entity, although all are part of a coordinated program. All operate under the Human Resources Center. Whereas Abilities, Inc. is self-sustaining, the educational and research activities are supported by grants, or, as in the case of the Human Resources School, tuition aid is obtained from our state Department of Education.

To understand us it is essential to understand this relationship. Even at times of industrial crises, when Abilities faces serious questions of loss of business, layoffs, and meeting payrolls, we cannot deny or turn from our purpose. We cannot change from an organization designed primarily to give realistic, meaningful employment to the disabled, and now to the retarded as well, into an industrial organization designed solely to make money. The programs of research, to record our experiences, to teach others; all these are essential in the work of changing the lives of the disabled.

A very dear friend of mine—a wealthy industrialist and a major stockholder in airline and chemical companies, fruit plantations and cattle ranches—wanted to help us over a critical period. I admired this man for his drive, his refusal to be defeated, his energy in whatever he attempted, and above all, for his good will, his desire to help.

Someone had sent him word that we were in serious trouble, which was certainly a fact. So he came in to see how he could help us. He even brought along his secretary to take notes on everything that was said. What he wanted to develop was a serious, ongoing, program.

He had never seen our operations before. I took him through the building and the various departments. Because of reduction in work, many of them were closed down. When we got back to my office, he said: "All right. We're going to get you out of this military contracting business. I'm going to put you in the plastics industry . . . this entire operation."

It was no joke, no visionary dream. He would help us obtain, he said almost casually, the volume of necessary equipment. I recall the image of this rugged, good-looking, youthful industrialist, standing there by my desk as his secretary jotted down notes on the various ideas and suggestions.

I said to him, "Why are you doing this? Certainly, you've got enough problems without adding ours, grateful as I am."

He looked at me with those steel-blue eyes of his

and said, "I only want to know that when Judgment Day comes and I'm standing there before the Lord and I see you over my shoulder—I want to know I have a chance."

"Well," I said, "That's a good enough reason for me."

So we agreed on his plan and he sent some of his highest executives and experts to survey our installation. They told us their boss had given them the entire picture: he was going to help us into plastics and we had better learn about plastics pretty fast; maybe we had better take a look at some of the plastic factories where they were turning out the raw material into manufactured articles.

Art and I agreed it was a wise suggestion. He and I and some of their experts went out in the snow and visited some of the molding plants. We went to back alleys in Brooklyn where plants were being operated at high production plastic levels. We saw good shops and bad, immaculate shops and filthy shops, shops turning out everything from plastic baby carriages to plastic teeth. All the shops were whirling. One thing they had in common, big or little, clean or dirty—they all appeared to be making money.

A second thing they had in common was highly sophisticated machinery, big rooms full of it, not small machines, but gigantic monstrous contraptions. We had people as a commodity; they had equipment. And the work went on around the clock, the machines chugged away twenty-four hours a day, turning out plastic toys, bags, and milk bottles, with trucks lined up at the back door to cart them off at frequent intervals; otherwise the workers would have been mill-

ing around up to their eyebrows in plastic products in
no time at all. This was what we were supposed to take
over and turn out, by the hundreds of thousands.

What was even more important, the machines did
all of this virtually by themselves. Staff was incidental.
Only a couple of fellows with what we call "golden
fingers" were required to keep the equipment running
smoothly. If anything got out of order, you were in real
trouble. Not only would the machines begin to turn
out milk bottles with holes in them, but you would
lose time, and time was basic to maximum production
and profit.

So you needed the machines first of all, then a few
golden fingers around just in case . . . and a few workers to sweep up the shavings and load the milk bottles
into trucks or the freight cars on the siding. In one
shop we found the plant being operated entirely by
refugees who had been brought in from a Displaced
Persons camp in Poland. They fed raw material, kept
an eye on the machines. Their most important assignment was to call the maintenance men if something
went wrong.

It was evident to Artie and me that this kind of
production was not for us. If we went into the plastics
field it was certain we could not need a staff of four
hundred people. All we would need would be a tight
little band of golden-fingered mechanics, not necessarily disabled, to watch over the machines and wet-
nurse them as required. We would make money because we would be turning out plastic items like crazy.
But we would not be proving anything we believed
in.

I wrote to the industrialist and explained our situation. He was, and is, one of my close friends and he understood exactly what I was saying. I could not— we could not—trade our real job of developing people. We were turning out a product the plastics companies hadn't yet learned how to make.

For us, however, there remained the problem of finding items our people *could* make. To help us find them, we had the advantage of future grants for research on specific needs in the field of rehabilitation medicine generally and in bioelectronic instrumentation specifically. Part of our mission was to seek out tools that would help doctors, and enable us to understand what was happening to disabled people at work. And this brings me to the story of Hans Krobath.

Hans is an electronics engineer and a gifted inventor. Born in Austria, he reluctantly served in the German armed forces as a technician. All he really wanted to do was to survive, to get out. His interests had nothing to do with Nazi politics; they were in equipment, electronic devices to run sound systems, high-fidelity amplifiers, tape recorders, public-address systems, communications, and radar.

All of this was his world. To Hans, America, where he came after the war on a visitor's visa, was the great dream personified. Soft spoken, mild of manner, he understood our great technical capacity; he wanted to be part of it, for he saw that here they turned technocracy not into dictatorships or wars of aggression against a neighbor, but into the work of saving lives, of benefiting humanity. In addition to the stimulation of our research needs, it was this interest in humanity (perhaps one would say the human machine), that led him into some research into bioelectronic instrumentation telemetry techniques and equipment, for example, to record the electrocardiogram, the pulse, the measurement of human fatique. We were, with our research team, constantly seeking new ways to determine if the disabled worker was becoming better or worse as he worked.

This decision led him to the Institute of Rehabilitation Medicine of New York University and it was there that he met Dr. Howard Rusk. To stay in America, and to bring his wife here, Hans had to have a full-time job. Dr. Rusk agreed to help. He called me and told me of the young scientist's interests and inventive genius. "Could you give him a job, Hank?" Rusk asked.

We were still in West Hempstead at that time, in the garage. There was no Human Resources Center at that time, and no school. And we had little work, only a few short-term contracts. Our biggest job was turning out the model plane assemblies. But we took Hans on, and his first assignment was to work out controls for model planes. He had, after all, been an aviation technician in the German Army of World War II.

But it was only a short time before the inventive genius of this man named Hans was turned to far more significant tasks.

As our West Hempstead operation developed, Hans became our Quality Control Supervisor.

At the same time he was learning the language, he was also learning every phase of our operation, and helping us to develop new machines and new methods for adapting normal manufacturing processes to the capacities of handicapped people. He was a genius at special tools and devices.

One of Hans' most important developments was to

come years later—as an answer, not primarily to our needs, but to the needs of all people.

It was in 1962, after we had moved into our new building at Albertson and the Human Resources Center was in full operation, that we received a grant from the Vocational Rehabilitation Administration, a division of the Department of Health, Education and Welfare. This grant was to enable us to carry on research in a field Hans described as "telemetering." We believed it could bring us into a whole new avenue of service and, at the same time, be of benefit to Abilities and its people.

Hans had a small research laboratory near our chapel; he was working in association with our research staff and our medical director, Dr. Slipyan, who has since died. At the outset, the main thrust of this work was statistical; we were seeking research data on the history of our workers and the changes that took place in them after they came into our operation. Dr. Slipyan was particularly concerned with cardiac workers and concentrated much of his effort on those individuals.

Hans' important contribution at this time was finding that there was no instrumentation available for research of this kind, no instrumentation that could transmit by telemetered remote signal the physiological reactions of individual workers, regardless of their disabilities, during working hours. It was important that the recording transmitters be not only miniaturized, but unencumbering to the worker. There was no means of obtaining data on physiological reactions in individuals as they worked, no small transmitters that would record heartbeat, respiration, and physical reactions that took place, that would add up to a total picture of an individual at work. It could be done in laboratories, but not at the work bench.

Without some kind of instrumentation, none of these reactions could be measured as the worker went about his rountine tasks. We talked about this problem, discussed it with Hans at length. Hans said he believed he could develop such a transmitter-recorder; he would make an experimental model. We were all excited at the idea. We thought: here perhaps is something not only of value to research, of untold worth to medicine in preserving human life, but also perhaps a marketable product.

Hans first developed an experimental model of an electrocardiogram amplifier. This amplifier was attached to the individual by a thin cable. The device was fed into an oscilloscope that showed the electrocardiogram. Hans later developed a miniature transmitter, about half the size of a pack of cigarettes, with battery power. This experimental model transmitted on ultra-high frequency waves to recorders set up in our laboratory. A worker with this instrument attached to him could go about his job in the plant and we would receive the data on his physical reactions on the laboratory receiving set. Hans stated of this first test: "I developed this experimental unit to see if it was possible in our industrial environment, in the midst of so many machines and electronic gear, to transmit the very low-level, delicate signals of an electrocardiogram. We established that these signals could be picked up in the factory and recorded by the receiver in the laboratory."

This was the beginning of our telemetering. What

the workers wore in these tests was actually a small amplifier and an equally small radio-transmitting station. This first machine employed only one transmitting channel. Later we obtained, through the Vocational Rehabilitation Administration, grants that permitted Hans to develop a multi-channel device that transmitted not just one type of information about the individual, but as many as twelve different physiological reactions. This second machine was still as small, but it was a twelve-channel, single-frequency transmitting package that could send out simultaneously over these channels information that might include the electrocardiogram, heart sounds, respiration, inspiration-expiration volume, flow rate, temperature of inspiration and expiration, skin resistance, skin temperature, electromyography, and electroencephalography.

All of this complex series of physiological data was channeled into a single frequency and transmitted in sequence at intervals of one twelve-thousandths of a second to the recording and receiving stations, where the data was unscrambled, collated, and recorded.

I and others in our organization, as well as a number of medical authorities working with us, regarded this complex instrumentation as a true contribution. We felt it could be of important use in many areas of medical and industrial research.

By means of this telemetering process we also learned much about our own disabled workers. We were able to show that many of them, far from becoming over-tired from performing our light-to-moderately-heavy industrial jobs, actually improved physically. We found also that where the work is lightest, the physiological changes are often greatest, due to psychological factors. The heart beat suddenly doubles—or slows, the blood pressure climbs, the respiration rate changes. Later tests, which we developed and carried out under controlled conditions, established fairly conclusively that these reactions were often the result of purely psychological factors—the appearance of a superior, the failure to achieve some minor goal, frustration, errors, changing of established routines—it could be any of these things.

The research into and development of this complex technical device, with all its rehabilitation and medical possibilities, was a time-consuming and costly enterprise. Much of the financing, as I have noted, came from federal grants, because the Division of Vocational Rehabilitation considered the potential findings of importance not only to disabled persons but to rehabilitation medicine and industrial medicine. From this came a second device, which many medical authorities told us would be of particular value in respiratory research, the electropneumotachometer.

So Hans and our research team of scientists had developed, at great cost in time, creative effort, and money, the telemetering system and this second device, which we felt might be used in every doctor's office because of its potential value in the swift diagnosis of respiratory and heart conditions. Both our medical advisors and our researchers at Human Resources Center were excited about it and its possibilities. We said to ourselves: what could be more logical than that Abilities and its people should become a supplier of medical instrumentation and electronic biomedical systems? It would be a natural result of our engineering expertise, our experience in manufacturing electronics, our fundamental humane concerns, and the general orientation of both our workers and management. And climaxing this, it would be of great benefit to the medical profession.

Our next step was to bring in someone to take over the distribution problem, to go out and market the devices. We did sell a few machines to a few Research Centers where they were used for further research, just as we had used them. Everything was exactly as we had believed: the instrumentation was needed, it was not available anywhere else, and it was an important contribution. What was lacking was acceptance, acceptance by the one group without whom we could not hope to make this a financial success—the medical people, the doctors, the hospital research staffs.

We learned a great deal from this blunder in marketing—which was precisely what it was. We learned that it isn't only need that counts, or even quality. When you set out to sell a product, you have to know the market so well that you can make reasonably accurate predictions in terms of sales. We were basically subcontractors. We were not marketing people. The companies for whom we worked did the selling, the aviation companies, the electronics companies.

How could we have made such a blunder? Weren't we as smart as other firms, other business people? I think the answer is that all firms make mistakes, that a business that doesn't make mistakes can't hope to grow because it isn't trying to keep up with new needs and ideas. We were not primarily businessmen or industrialists. When Artie and I opened up operations in that West Hempstead garage over a decade ago, we were neophites. We had learned a lot fast, and we were lucky in plenty of ways, for we survived and grew.

Now we were learning new things. And one thing we learned was that you can't change the medical profession in a year or two or three. You can't change ingrained habits and ideas by coming out with a new device. You don't get acceptance of new biomedical equipment until years of research have taken place, until papers are written and published, until the profession approves of and seeks your product. You don't get acceptance for new instrumentation until all the facts and figures are in and the product has stood all the challenges possible in a profession that involves its use daily, and at any moment of any hour, in determining the issues of life and death. We should have known that but we didn't. You also don't sell it just because it's good. You need marketing and merchandizing research.

One medical friend of mine put it in these terms: "Your machine is like something out of the future, Hank. One day it may be accepted and used. But now you are ahead of us, miles ahead. The instrumentation and measurements are magnificent. But how many doctors would know what the physiological measurements mean or how to use them?"

Of course, we were discouraged as this situation unfolded before us, at the collapse of our high hopes that the telemetering program in addition to our research findings would lead us into a whole new marketing area. Now we knew that it would not do anything of the kind. However valuable we might find the instrumentation in our own research at the Human Resources Center and with our workers at Abilities, we

knew we faced a long haul to get it accepted elsewhere. We would have to consider a ten-year investment of time and work with research doctors before
we could hope to have our instrumentation accepted
widely as a medical tool.

The blunt truth was that we were swept up with
enthusiasm and had not explored the marketing problem properly. We had not coldly and methodically
surveyed outside expert opinions to make sure we
were on the right track. The concepts of marketing
and merchandizing were more than a little new to us.

In all our shining hopes we had gone forth, on our
first real foray into the non-subcontracting world. The
result was rough blow. We still faced the grim economic picture on Long Island, with more and more
firms closing down. We still had no product with
which to enter the direct consumer market.

It was a bad moment for us. We were jolted, we
were angry, we were disappointed, we were concerned. But looking back on it, perhaps it was one of
the best things that could have happened to us, because it did awaken all of us at Abilities and Human
Resources Center to the hard cold facts of the competitive business world. We were forced into battle, a
battle that we could not win on any grounds except
know-how in every phase of industrial operation, from
choosing the right kind of products for a diversification program to manufacturing and marketing them
successfully.

When we had started out we had prayed for a
chance to work, prayed for equal opportunity at a
machine, asking no handouts, only the chance to show
that we could succeed.

Well, we had the chance. They were giving us exactly what we wanted—no dimes, no quarter, unless we produced products they wanted to buy.

The road ahead was challenging and perilous, and strewn, peculiarly enough, with glittering glass.

## 8

## *Glass and Dreams*

The gleaming pleasure dome of carved glass that was designed to shelter Abilities and its people from any further financial storms came into being in a curious fashion, by way of a phone call from a stranger.

The call came to Art Nierenberg who by then held the title of executive vice-president. The caller suggested carved glass as a consumer product Abilities could manufacture and sell direct to America's stores.

This was what we still desperately needed, we decided—a product of our own. This was the core of our plan for diversification; something, anything, we could make and sell ourselves. Not just beads or trinkets— something important, needed, a thing people wanted and would pay for. I had told Art and the others: "If you run into any opportunity, let me know. If it stands a chance, we'll consider it."

Art wheeled into my office that afternoon in a bright cloud of excitement. "Hank," he demanded, "what do you know about engraved glass?"

I was about to tell him I knew nothing about glass

when he plunged into his story. A man had phoned and suggested that we get into engraved-glass production, making articles for direct consumer sale. "We've been looking for this for months, Hank," he reminded me.

The idea was that we would buy the glass forms uncut and undecorated—water glasses and wine glasses, old-fashioned and high-ball glasses, glass ash trays, bottles, vases—and decorate them with delicate carving. "Engraved glass is all the rage. We could develop processes that would enable us to turn out glasses cheaply and as beautiful as anything you can buy today."

"Who does it? Where do we get the people who know how to carve on glass?"

"Get them? We've got 'em. Our own people. Including our MR workers. They've got talent and skill and they can be trained." I could see Art's enthusiasm in his expression, hear it in his voice. "Look, for the first time Abilities could have a product!" he was saying.

To us, this idea had great possibilities. Glass items were stable rather than seasonal. If they were dropped, they usually smashed; if they were smashed, they had to be replaced. The more Art and I discussed it, the more certain I was that this suggestion had validity. It could be a great venture for us; it could be an answer to jobs for the mentally retarded whom we wanted to help.

By the time I was down in Washington at the Department of Labor, again seeking aid on our training programs, I had a meager background on how and what we might do with glass. We would use a system of "multiple-hand" production, that is, individual artisans working with mechanisms that enabled the worker to turn out five carvings at once, each as perfect as the original. "We call it 'pantograph kinomechanism,'" I explained to the group. "It is something new and it will enable us to produce magnificent carved-glass products at prices three or four times cheaper than the usual market price. It will allow us to train and provide jobs for many retarded and disabled workers."

"Pantograph kinomechanisms" was actually my own descriptive term for the new devices, so it was not surprising that none of the people had heard of them before. Even Art was not quite certain of what it meant. He kept asking me to spell it and I couldn't get it to come out the same twice in a row. But they listened very attentively and respectfully to my explanation of the process and the kind of beautiful glassware we could turn out, using the mentally retarded as the basic skilled-labor force of the program. The process had to be developed. We believed it could be done.

"How do you know the MR's are capable of this sort of thing?" I was asked.

"Because we can simplify the operation with studies. They have a much higher than usual level of attention," I explained. "They like to stay in one place, to work long over a detailed job that often would bore a more alert person. In addition, they seem to delight in opportunities to be creative."

I went on to say that we believed we were lucky to have a special work force of this kind who we were convinced would respond particularly well to training in this field. We believed that with reasonable effort the engraving techniques could be developed. They listened and asked questions and then they said they would go along with us: we would have funds to train these people and develop the glass-engraving process.

It was more than a great victory; we were, we felt, started on the way. We would set up our own sales staff, and we would go directly to the stores of America with a fine product that people wanted and used steadily, and at a price well under the competition. It seemed a hard combination to beat. Meanwhile we would be training workers for jobs elsewhere.

We bought some unmarked glass forms from a wholesale house and had begun experimenting with the process when we had another telephone call. This time the call came from the president of one of the nearby manufacturing concerns, the Ford Instrument Company. He wanted to tell us of an inventor who was near retirement, in fact, was approaching his eightieth year, but who remained extremely active. He had developed a series of satisfactory kinomechanisms used in aerial photography. We invited this inventor to join us, because we realized that the mechanism itself was a key factor and needed much in the way of development, just as our MR's and other workers needed training both in design and actual glass-carving techniques. The mechanism was like an automatic check writer; we could carve several glasses at once.

In those early stages we turned out several experimental ash trays bearing the Seal of the President of the United States, and when I went down to a meeting of the Presidential Panel of the retarded I took a couple of these unfinished pieces with me as examples of what we were attempting.

I showed them to Eunice Shriver and she took one look at them and said, "Oh, I'd like to show these to the President." She did show them to him and shortly afterward she told me, "I think the President would like a couple of these ash trays for his home."

Then she said a little later (I had the feeling she had discussed the project with the President), "Do you think you'll go ahead with it? Do you think it is good for the retarded?"

I said, "Yes, I think it is, and I think we can fit it all together. We're working on it, anyway."

We continued with our experiments, and brought in the elderly inventor. At one point, when the project seemed to bog down, we turned to our real inventive backstop—Hans. Hans pitched in and helped to perfect the mechanism by which, from one original glass carving, five copies could be reproduced, all with absolute accuracy.

By the fall of 1963, we felt that we had the mechanical problems licked, the workers trained, and we were about to move into full-scale operation. Suddenly, we found ourselves in the midst of broken glass and broken dreams—not we alone, nor even America, but the whole world.

On November 22, 1963, President John Fitzgerald Kennedy was assassinated in Dallas, Texas.

Despite the death of the President—the shocking unreal reality—the world had to go on, even our small projects at Abilities and Human Resources Center. And they did, including the glass project which now moved into the final stage, merchandising.

Once again I have to admit frankly that we made serious errors, based primarily on what we did not know about merchandising. As one example, we retained a sales agent who had previously sold similar products to stores throughout the country. He told us we could not price ourselves too high or we would miss the mass markets. Acting on his advice, we cut the wholesale prices to levels he felt proper and decided we could make it up inside the shop, by reducing the cost of operations. Unfortunately, there was no room for cost reduction, no fat to cut out.

Moreover, the orders we began to get were few, spare, and varied. This store wanted that design, but with changes here or there. The next wanted the whole thing in blue or pink. With our vast inexperience in consumer merchandising, every buyer seemed to us like an art director of a museum, exercising his or her own tastes in engraved glass. When we tried to please a few, as in the old fable, we wound up pleasing none.

We were taking orders for four of these and twelve of those, we were trying to build inventory, and we were also still working on the mechanism and the entire engraving process. It was far from perfected. Little of what we had been told of what we had expected of our original process worked out under high-pressure usage. We were mass producing what is called barware—engraved highball glasses and old-fashioned glasses. Meanwhile, through our national distribution company, we were dealing with department-store buyers, and each individual buyer was insisting on her personal choice. As one of our MR's put it succinctly, "One of them wants bluebirds and the other wants carnations."

The orders we expected to pour in came in driblets. The problems of production eventually cleared up, but the problems of distribution and acceptance remained. There was no profit. The pricing problem was chaos. More and more we began to question ourselves, to realize that we had too little understanding of direct-to-consumer sales techniques.

I assume there were some on our board, and perhaps throughout the company, who might have decided that the wisest thing to do would be to abandon the whole glass project as a failure. Yes, we had made a few beautiful pieces of carved glassware and had helped to perfect a process that was obviously valuable economically. However, it was apparently not our carved glass of tea, not our vase of fulfillment. The research and errors had been very costly.

Nonetheless, we did not abandon the process entirely. We continued working at it, turning out glassware to fill the orders that came in, but we knew we would have to find new ways, new ideas, new production approaches, to fulfill our needs and goals.

We were not looking for an absolutely sure thing that couldn't fail. As always, in dealing with the disabled and the retarded, I have insisted that they must not look for security. This is true for all men, in fact, whatever their physical or mental condition. Security, as such, does not exist, certainly not in the freedom one finds in America. Our nation was founded on risk. There's a calculated risk in everything we do, just as there was in every stage of our development as a nation. We have always had scientists who were not afraid of truth, thinkers who were not afraid of progress, and dreamers who were not afraid of action, or of failure.

I cite this fact here because it is pertinent to the time when the glass dream could have been shattered. That

*Air view of Human Resources Center. Abilities is at upper right of complex; Human Resources School is at left. Beyond large parking area are lawns, paths and trees of school playground.*

*One section of the wide-aisle work area of Abilities. Cleanliness and modern work-flow methods are key efficiency factors in meeting production goals.*

*A close-up look at another area. In foreground is testing equipment. Note material storage bins that help keep production flowing smoothly.*

*Paralyzed limbs do not impair manual dexterity. Here a worker at Abilities prepares electric wire for cable assembly.*

*Skilled men and women engaged in highly technical electronic production, an important speciality at Abilities.*

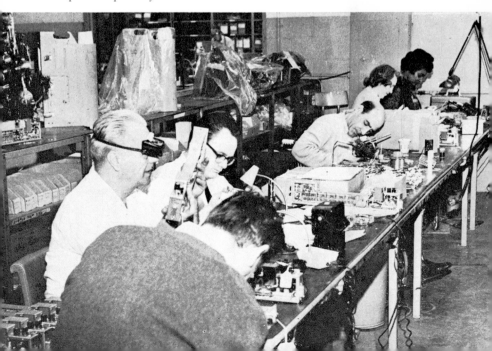

At Abilities packaging
center in Syosset, L.I.
seriously disabled
handle large packages
for shipment.

S.   *l and label operation*
must n.   *recise specifications,*
e?   *when the worker has a*
      *hand with no fingers.*

Disabled workers
fabricate cases for
military bomb racks.

*Audio-visual training. Kodachrome film image on machine shows him what to do while voice on sound track gives him step-by-step directions in assembling complicated equipment.*

*Inventor and project director, Hans Krobath, working at telemetering equipment by which physical reactions and energy levels are studied electronically. Federal funds and private foundation grants helped to pay for the research that made telemetering a reality.*

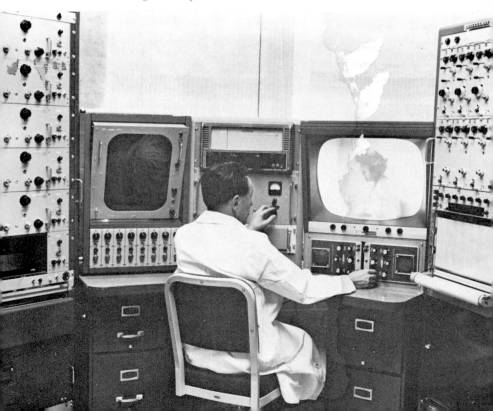

*Deposits and withdrawals are posted in passbooks in Abilities banking operation, just : at any bank.*

*The new world of d ta-processing equipment opens up many opportunities for workers.*

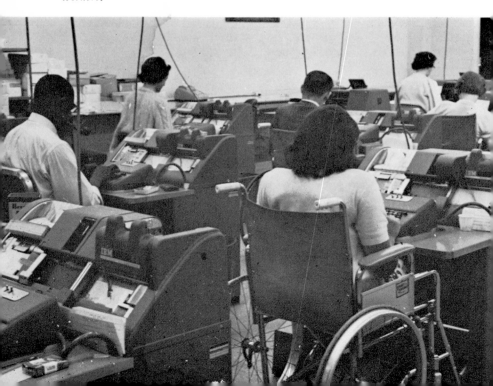

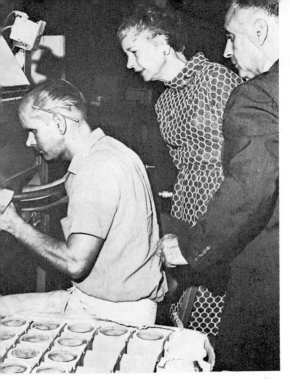

Mrs. W. Willard Wirtz, wife of Secretary of Labor Willard Wirtz, watches glass-etching process while Henry Viscardi, Jr., explains engraving techniques. President Johnson selected Abilities glassware as official White House gifts for distinguished visitors from other lands.

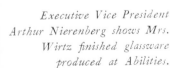

Executive Vice President Arthur Nierenberg shows Mrs. Wirtz finished glassware produced at Abilities.

A bud glass engra[v]ed at Abilities is presented to disabled worker at Sun Industries, Beppu, during Henry Viscardi's tour of Japan and Korea.

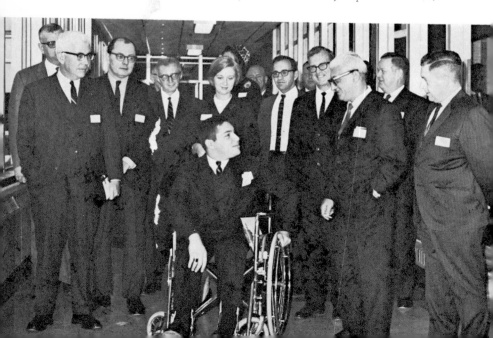

*Suzanne Szasz*

A kiss for **Mr. Viscardi**—from a little girl at the Human Resources School for severely disabled children.

Leaders of commerce and industry, studying employment problems of disabled and retarded, on guided tour of Human Resources Center under direction of Tour Director, Richard Rosenbaum (center in wheelchair).

Hun▢ ▢esources School was built to accommodate ultimately two hundred boys and gir▢ ▢isabled to be accepted in other schools. Every room in school opens on a garde▢.

When it rains, the ▢ ▢cially-built school bus pulls up to the covered path . . . so the children won't ▢ ▢t drenched getting to classes.

*Overhead screen projections, more*
*convenient than blackboards, help*
*disabled students participate in class-*
*room work. Adjustable desk tops are*
*another special aid to students.*

*Suzanne Szasz*

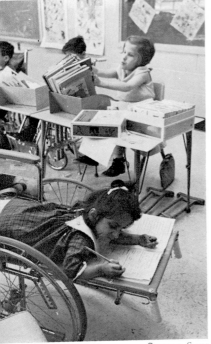

*She can live and work and learn in a*
*schoolroom on a litter, as well as she could*
*in a wheelchair.*

*Suzanne Szasz*

*Suzanne Szasz*

*A little boy whose fingers do not*
*open or close learns to write his*
*name ... to prepare himself for life.*

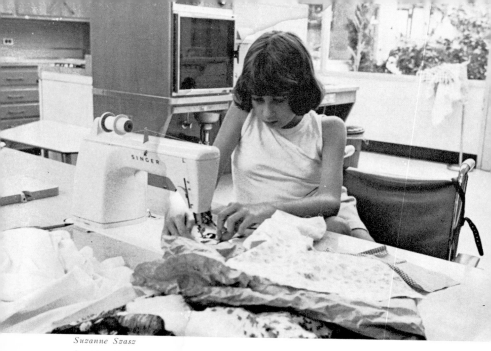

Suzanne Szasz

In the Laboratory for Everyday Living, a young girl learns to sew. Home economics is taught in this unique laboratory to help the disabled learn to get into a bathtub unaided, or make a bed, or bathe an infant.

Suzanne Szasz

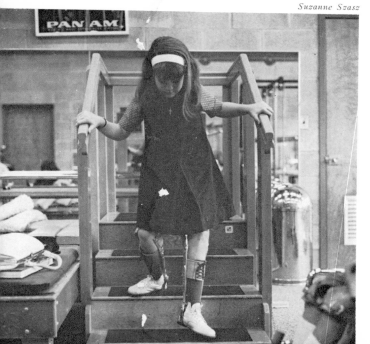

In physical education program, a little girl takes a few important steps in the learning process. There will be many other steps to learn in everyday life. . . .

The Greenhouse, the hub around which the Human Resources School is designed. Here the children help grow plants. It is also the special province of the school's parrot. Note lovely statue of child in foreground.

Presenting Abilities award for long-term service to Abilities and its goals.

*Action in the afternoon . . . the young have fun like everybody else. Special ramps aid children and adults entering and leaving water.*

*Mr. Viscardi and youngsters from the school in the Human Resources pool.*

*It's a sure strike—or is it? —for one lad, using Abilities' special bowling equipment while his opponent waits to strike back.*

*Indoor hockey . . . and the kids play rough. The youngsters love the competition and it strengthens their faith in themselves.*

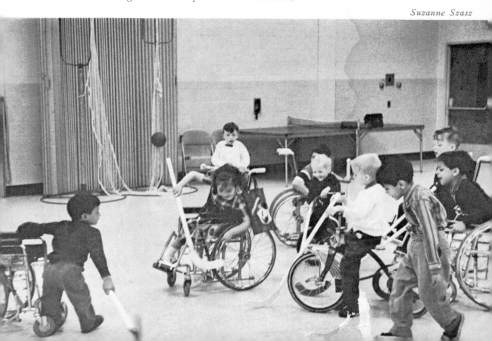

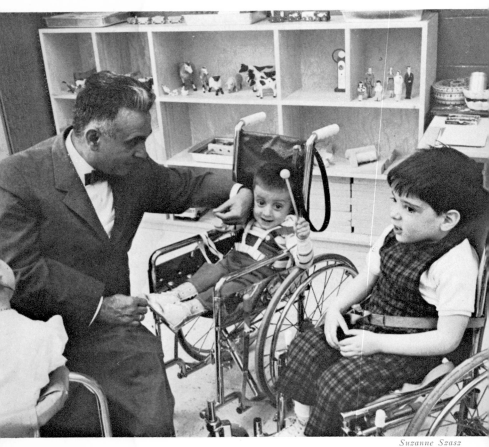

*Suzanne Szasz*

*A boy in a wheelchair listens to Hank Viscardi's watch and beats time with a drum stick while the other children look on. In part because of the Human Resources School, time for these children has meaning and direction in their lives.*

there was a way to use the process and market it profitably, I was sure. That we would find it, I was also sure. That we would not retreat and abandon it was equally a certainty.

It was not a failure. The glassware itself was magnificent. More than that, the MR's and disabled who had learned to carry out this process had developed in ways we had not anticipated. They had come to us only a month before as half-lost souls, capable perhaps, but useless because they lacked training. No one would give them a chance to try to do things they had never been considered capable of doing before.

All the time we had been working on the problem of manufacturing, distributing, and marketing our beautiful glassware, we had been forging futures for mentally retarded young men and women. It was a magnificent training ground for developing their skills and their sense of responsibility both to themselves and to their jobs. They began to understand the concept of quality control, of the need to meet not only schedules, but also the levels of quality demanded. We had made workers out of mentally retarded people in an artistic field that was for many a springboard to jobs outside our plant. We didn't like losing these workers we had trained, but we were proud of their progress, proud that they could reach out in the world beyond our doors. Many were trained, then placed in outside jobs.

In the midst of our concern over the carved-glass situation, even as we were reaching out for new proposals and approaches, I recall one incident that touched me deeply. It involved the ash trays for President Kennedy.

They had been finished just after the assassination

and I had put them away. They were crystal and on them we had engraved the Great Seal of The President of the United States. During this time the Kennedy family had remained to a large extent away from the public. Then, when they began to come out of their seclusion somewhat, about three months after President Kennedy's death, I learned that Eunice and Sargent Shriver were dedicating a new wing at the University of Chicago for research on mental retardation.

Routinely, as a member of the President's Panel on Mental Retardation, I had received an invitation. Normally, I wouldn't have gone, but this time I flew out to Chicago and I went through the receiving line. I doubt if anyone knew who I was; it was one of those affairs where everybody shows up, all the top educational people. A man stood beside Eunice, asking each guest his name, so he could present him. I said, "I'm Dr. Viscardi," which was true. (And I have some honorary degrees to prove it!)

When they introduced me, Eunice looked up. "Hank Viscardi!" she exclaimed and reached out her hand. "I'm pleased to see you. What are you doing out here?"

I said, "I came because I have something in my briefcase that I want you to see."

She called to her husband, "Sarge! Here's Hank!"

I said hello to Sargent Shriver and then Eunice dropped out of the receiving line and brought me over to a corner. "What have you got?" she asked.

I opened my briefcase and took out the crystal ash tray engraved with the Great Seal of the President of the United States.

"It's very pretty," Eunice said.

"Do you remember it?" I asked.

She said, "I surely do."

"I brought it as a gift for you and Sarge," I told her. "I hope you'll accept it."

Eunice Shriver is not usually a highly emotional person on the surface, but I could see that now she was deeply moved. She called Shriver over and said, "Look, Sarge. Hank brought this as a gift for us. Isn't that wonderful?"

Shriver nodded and said, "It is, indeed, Hank. I'm so grateful."

Then Eunice said, "As I recall it, there were two. What will you do with the other one?"

I explained that it was to be given to President Johnson.

She nodded, telling me this was right, that she understood, and we went back to the receiving line. The second ash tray was presented to Mrs. Johnson at a ceremony arranged by Secretary of Labor Wirtz and his charming wife at the Department of Labor.

I didn't even stay for lunch at the dedication in Chicago. The mission was done. I turned around and took the next plane back to New York.

## 9

## That Wonderful Balancing Machine

The balancing machine is a symbol to us at Abilities, because it was so much a part of the struggle—the victories and the setbacks. We were a well-organized group in full-fledged operation; we still had enough business to keep us alive and to keep a lot of our equipment in operation. It was the downward trend that bothered us, and the need to build for the future. Much of what we did had to be opportunistic, we had to use every challenge as an advance, every development of today as a hope for a breakthrough tomorrow. If the carved glass was not the immediate answer, if telemetering and the electropneumotachometer were long-range projects on which we could profit only with patience and years, we agreed to keep them going at a nominal level and direct our main efforts to another area on the battlefront. This was our decision, even though it tempted us, momentarily, into a thread of giant turbines and power plants!

In this battle, Hans Krobath was one of our most loyal and important individuals. For his was, and is, the creative mind, searching out and finding not only the heart of the problem but also, where possible, the solution. To Hans, we owe the wonderful balancing machine and its unique history at Abilities.

We were turning out motors for fan mechanisms and other rotating components. Hans found that we needed a better quality control, particularly to be sure that these motors, which have speeds often of many thousands of revolutions per minute, were properly balanced, that no part of the whirling mechanism was heavier than another or out of line. Otherwise, vibrations begin and quickly tear the motors apart.

Machines to test the exact balance characteristics of such motors—and larger rotating components as well —are very expensive. Furthermore, in dealing with extremely small motors, the instrument that touches the mechanism in order to make the measurement could damage the parts it touches. Hans told me, "What we need is a machine to test balance that does not have to touch anything. It has to be done by sensors. It has to be done electronically."

To my lay mind, this sounded as though we would have to come up with a trick of modern alchemy. But Hans set to work to find out a practical answer. He made his laboratory tests and in a comparatively short time he had developed a truly extraordinary device which we patented and which we called "No Con," because it enabled us to make accurate balancing measurements electronically without any physical contact.

As Hans described it to some of our directors, "Perfect balance is important, you see, in such things as these tiny armatures we make for General Electric.

After the armature is wound, it has to be balanced. We must know that the finished product is not loud and doesn't rattle. This is vital because the life of the product, the bearings of the motor, depends on proper balance."

This was actually Hans' first venture into major industrial-machine design. What he had developed was a machine with electronic probes that measure vibration, or, as Hans describes it, measures "displacement from a steady state." The machine operates by an electronic eye that senses the presence of metallic substance in front of its "sensing face," which is brought within a quarter of an inch of any rotating part, a resolver or motor, without touching that part. It records not only that there is a vibration, but by means of an indexing electron protractor, will pinpoint where the vibration is, on that whirling part. When you stop the motor, the machine shows you exactly where the fault lies, and corrective action can be taken, extra weight taken away, to reduce vibration to an absolute minimum.

Hans' invention was a highly technical one, not a glamourous innovation like the electric light or the television set, but a contribution to industry, another of the behind-the-scenes workhorse gadgets, without which glamourous developments never get off the drawing board.

Because No Con can also be used in probing thicknesses in almost any kind of product, its uses industrially are far wider in scope and potential than either Hans or anyone else in Abilities anticipated when we first developed it as a quality control measurement for our own use.

On a visit to our plant, a group of top officials of an electric company noticed the balancing machine and appeared fascinated by its possibilities. They had some problems of their own in measuring imbalance in some of their turbines. Could we help? We thought we could, even though their problems sounded much larger than any we had ever dealt with before. Hans and some of his aides went up to New England to look over the situation in one of the divisions of their vast industrial complex.

Later, I went with Hans to a plant just outside of Boston, where the first test in connection with their giant turbines would be held. They will build you a turbine big enough to generate electricity for a whole city, or a great new ship, if you want to order one. I don't exactly know how much these things cost, but I know it takes a couple of years to get delivery on them, because they have to be done with the greatest kind of industrial know-how and skill and constant testing. And they have to be balanced all the time, just as our motors at Albertson do, because they too are constantly spinning at so many thousands of revolutions per minute, and if anything went wrong, it would, as one of the men put it "sure raise hell." When they revved it up the noise was terrifying, more piercing than a jet plane taking off.

The techniques they employed in the balancing process took months. They were using some kind of hand probe—it looked like a streamlined broom stick to my non-technical eyes—to feel out the vibrations and record any that seemed off-center. Hans figured out that our No Con probe could balance this giant in a brief period of time, because it functioned, not mechanically, but electronically. But new ideas have to fight their way, even when they can prove themselves in ten minutes.

This is especially true, I have noted, in companies that are highly departmentalized. New ideas or new methods quite properly have to be fitted into established procedures and rules and regulations. We ran into one impediment after another. Things that Hans needed to show how the job would work simply weren't set up. Or a hole had to be drilled, and they had to call a hole-driller, because no one else could drill a hole; unfortunately, the hole-driller wouldn't be available for half an hour, and when the hole-driller finally did show up, he had to go back to get his drill. By then it was time for lunch and everybody had to stop.

After many exchanges, we finally just said to them, in effect, "Look friend, it isn't working out, you keep your turbines and we'll keep our electronic measuring instrumentation, and no hard feelings on either side." And reluctantly we left.

It wasn't entirely their fault—or ours. But it was our fault really, in a way that had nothing to do with the machine itself. We simply didn't know what to do with a product. We didn't know how to find a market. If we found the market, we didn't know how to sell the product. A good idea was wasted in our hands. We never seemed to talk to the right people.

Another company heard about this machine of ours and sent some of their people to talk with us about it. They were interested in the marketing possibilities, but there were a great many things they wanted to know first. We didn't know where it would lead, but we were delighted with their interest and perfectly willing to talk. Talk we did—for months and months, in conferences at Abilities or their offices or wherever the needs took us. It was a protracted operation, and we invested a great deal of hope and faith (and dreams of ultimate success) in the discussions. And, of course, at the same time we were running a work center, a research center, and raising hundreds of thousands of dollars—this, primarily, to build the Human Resources School. It was a busy time!

But not all dreams come to fulfillment. You have to be able to accept that and pick yourself up. I recall our final conference with these people; we had worked so hard, we had built our ideas and our faith to a point where this time we were certain we had an avenue to marketing. Then came this conference, at a new motel near the airport. This was the moment they had picked to tell us the product wasn't for them; they had tested the market and it wasn't ready. The device hadn't reached a point where it could be considered a volume product. They simply weren't interested.

This was a grim evening for us, but so casual for them. That was the kind of ball game we were in. You won and you lost. We had a wonderful dinner in a lovely restaurant, but the food turned to charcoal in my throat.

From that company's point of view they were right. And we were, again, showing our naivete in these matters. We had been too sure. Hans, of course, had his other developments that he was simultaneously working on, other inventions in the bio-instrumentation field. Inventive genius is not to be stopped; other instrumentations in this field are even now, as I write, in the process of development in Hans' laboratory.

But it was at this point that we began to realize that

a total about-face was essential. Our picture required analysis. There was success, there was failure, there were setbacks. We had been reaching out ever since the late 1950's, ever since the subcontracting had begun to cut back. We knew that a certain amount of business would continue. We knew that we could obtain other types of work, automated jobs. The plastic milk bottle world was waiting and they were willing for us to try. But we knew also that automation would not give enough employment to provide for our people.

The banking program was a success, in full operation, and expanding. We were moving into new aspects in this field, to areas of service bureau and data processing on an expanded scale. Our research projects in the Human Resources Center were progressing well, the results being received with favor by the government agencies and private foundations and the grants-in-aid being considered for additional projects. As an example of the kind of productive research we engaged in at the Human Resources Center, I would like to quote the following from one of our own official reports on our work:

The Exploratory and Evaluative Research in the Vocational Adjustment of the Handicapped was carried out utilizing the unique facilities of the Institute, which is the research, training, and educational affiliate of Abilities, Inc. The facilities of Human Resources Research and Training Institute, which include 4,000 square feet of research, classroom, library, and recreational space, were built at a cost of approximately $1,000,000 of which $195-000 was received under a grant from the Health

Research Facilities Branch of the National Institute of Health.

The areas designated for pure and applied research include laboratories equipped for medical research, biochemical investigation, reception and recording of physiological and psychological telemetric data, and comprehensive diagnostic testing. These are supplemented by an X-Ray room with facilities for X-Ray examination and reproduction, a dental facility with ancillary dental research equipment, a research ophthalmological facility, and general medical examination and evaluation rooms. Additional areas are equipped for research in medical electronics, prosthetics, orthetics, and a variety of projects for the mentally retarded.

The psychosocial research program is conducted in rooms designed for interviews, observation, and small and large group testing. An area is also provided for data processing and statistical analyses in medical, psychosocial, and telemetric research. . . .

These were the programs of research that we were carrying on at the same time we were carrying on work projects, employing hundreds of the disabled and the retarded, trying to hold the whole operation intact, trying to establish ourselves on a firm and stable foundation for now and the future, trying to find a way through to a program of real diversification and development of real consumer products of our own.

All of this was being challenged in the Abilities operations by the cutting back of work in some areas, by our own shortcomings in the field of consumer marketing, and by our lack of funds. This last was becoming an increasing, almost crushing, burden. Payments on our mortgage, loans, and short-term financing all still had to be met.

We had asked to be allowed to live like all other human beings, and to be considered on ability, not disability.

And the world had answered us in kind. We were facing the competition and we would win or lose on merit and nothing else.

Sometimes it takes blunders, to which all of us are prone, to open our eyes.

One, for me, was a special meeting in Washington. It was of extreme importance to us, and to our research program, for it involved the renewal of a long-range grant for approximately half a million dollars. Without that renewal, much of our research on behalf of the disabled and the retarded would have to be curtailed, so we wanted to put our best foot forward when we made our presentation in Washington.

We had made a film of some importance in the field of vocational rehabilitation, and Mary Switzer, the administrator of the whole Vocational Rehabilitation Program, was anxious to see it. In fact, on the day we were to show it, she arranged to fly back to Washington from a conference many miles distant, in order to see this film.

I too flew down to Washington for this important meeting. In my briefcase my secretary had dutifully placed the film that Mary Switzer was so eager to see.

When I got to Washington, however, I found a message from my office waiting for me. They had given me the wrong film.

It was too late to stop Mary Switzer, who was already winging her way to see how efficient and effective we were and what great things we were doing, and she was, I am certain, disappointed. I didn't even get to see her. I knew I made too much of the disappointment. In her kindly understanding way, she was disappointed but no more than that. But the entire day's conferences with her staff had gone poorly. My presentations had sounded weak. They fell flat, it seemed to me. To let her down was the final blow to me. It was a dismal day.

I felt a chill in the Washington air, a deserved chill, I might add. The whole staff of this office had been invited to see this film; the Commissioner had told them it was an important thing and that they would want to see it; it was a documentary film made by the Japanese for release on TV in Japan. Parts had been taken at VRA while we were presenting a demonstration there. Miss Switzer and her staff were in the film.

And here all I had was a roll of film about something that had nothing whatever to do with this subject and which we could not even show.

I caught the plane back to New York. When I reached home, my wife Lucile took one look at me and said, "I won't ask you how it went."

I said, "Let's have a drink before dinner."

"Good idea. Anyway, dinner's not quite ready."

I went into the pantry for our cocktail fixings and closed the door—in our pantry, closing the door puts out the light. I just couldn't face her. I stayed in there, trying to compose myself. This was in the midst of all our assorted problems, when things seemed to have reached low, low tide: Abilities and its debts and its need for new markets and new products; the school and its new and exciting but everlasting challenges in terms of funds and staff and buildings and the neighbors (with their sound, healthy, two-legged kids), who still objected to the fact that we were nearby.

All of it was piling in on us. And this today had been something important, a turning point that could have helped solve at least the research and training problems. Only it was washed out.

Lucile opened the door of that darkened pantry and I was in tears, not for myself, but for all of them, for this whole dream of ours. "Hank, what happened?" she asked.

"I blew it," I told her. "I blew the whole bit—a half million dollars for research."

"Hank," she said, "you didn't blow it. Mix a drink. We have a good dinner almost ready."

Funny. It was something my mother used to say to me. My mother is one of those wonderful old-fashioned women. No matter what happened—you could fracture your arm—and Mama would still say, "I'll fix you a nice dinner, you'll feel better." And here was Lucile saying almost those same words.

I went into the kitchen and began to mix the drinks.

But I didn't enjoy that dinner, no matter how wonderful it was, and Lucile is a truly magnificent cook. We didn't talk about any of this to our four young daughters; no reason to give them something to worry over that wasn't their problem at all.

But afterward, as I usually do, I read to my youngest one, and, also as usual, I stayed there beside her until she fell asleep. But that night, sitting beside her bed after reading, after she dozed off, her hand still in mine, I felt a great surge of emotion. I was overcome by a sense of inadequacy, not in relation to her or my other daughters as a father, because I knew I was adequate in that, but inadequacy toward the ideals of Abilities and Human Resources and the Human Resources School, toward all the people I loved.

There was a nagging question stirring my emotions. The question was of deceit, not other people's, but my own. Had I deceived all of them—the board, our supporters, Washington—and myself too, by trying to indicate that I could swing this project? That all they had to do was trust in me and the whole thing would work out the way it should, the way everyone wanted?

Nobody had forced me to do it. I designed it, I developed it, I made it grow. Some of my board members who were more conservative than others had said, "Look, why this, why Human Resources, why the school? Isn't Abilities enough?" As far back as 1952, when we wanted to break out of the first garage, the board had at first refused its approval and I had to go back and convince them that this was the next great step, the Abilities building in Albertson.

I must have dozed off in these moments, sitting there beside my sleeping daughter, my mind a jumble of thoughts. Foremost among them was the feeling that perhaps I had betrayed all of them by taking this road, the path to glory, not my glory but glory for all the others. But I was the one who had insisted on it. I was the head of this small army of the disabled and retarded, marching them down the long twisting road to someplace. And now, suddenly, in that moment of self-questioning and doubt, the question became where were we headed? If I had created the image and laid down the course line for this journey, had I mapped out more than I or the others could achieve? Should I begin to cut back to safer, less challenging ground? Or, even more basic, was I the wrong man for this leadership? Oughtn't I to face up to the possibility that what we needed was a more competent man to bail us out of the thousands of problems that were closing in?

I put these questions down here now, not rhetorically, but because they were the actual questions I asked myself that night.

I seemed to awaken then, in the darkness. I could hear the deep breathing of my little girl. The house was silent. I was sure the rest of the family had gone to bed, the girls dawdling as they usually do, putting up their hair and all the hundred and one other things they must do before you drive them under the covers.

Then Lucile came into the room—it was dark, except for a night light—and opened the window and said to me, "Don't you think you'd better come to bed now, Hank?"

She knew. She knew the disturbing thoughts that were coursing through me. I didn't need to say one word.

I remember undressing and getting into bed and I recall how she came over and put her arms around me and said, "Look, it isn't the end. Not for you or Abilities or anybody. Hank, you know it could be the beginning? If we work on it together, do a little praying over it . . ."

And she was right, I thought. It had to be a new beginning. We had to face ourselves, all of us in Abilities and Human Resources. We had to re-examine what we were doing and how we were doing it, what was wrong or right with us. We had to look at ourselves and our organization, our virtues, our mistakes, our potentials. We had to have business answers that made sense. And realistic management answers that added up to victory.

Lucile was asleep beside me now. But I was very much awake. And in my mind, in that darkness, I seemed to feel Lucile's pulsing words: "it could be the beginning . . ."

Wives are so often right.

## 10

## *Command Decisions*

‖‖‖‖‖‖‖‖‖‖‖‖‖‖‖‖‖‖‖‖‖‖‖‖‖‖‖‖‖‖‖‖‖‖‖‖‖‖‖‖‖‖‖‖‖‖‖‖‖‖‖‖‖‖‖‖‖‖‖‖‖‖‖‖‖‖‖‖‖‖‖‖‖‖‖‖‖‖‖‖‖‖

The Washington fiasco was not so much a crisis as a sign of impending crisis. We did ultimately receive that grant; we were not as badly off as we had thought. But it had been a warning, telling us that we had to take action, as an enterprise; we had to change course, we had to examine the past and present and make some realistic plan for the future.

Earnings were slipping in proportion to our retreating subcontracts. Our former total gross earnings had been reduced approximately one-third. In the Abilities operation we were fast reaching a financial point of no return. We had to solve the financial problems or lose Abilities.

I was not prepared to lose it. Too much of my life, all of our lives, had gone into it. But I knew that we had to examine our experience and analyze ourselves. Only within ourselves would we find the answers. Once before, when the war was over, I had turned from the disabled but had been drawn back. I could leave for a much better job anytime. There were con-

stant offers. But what would become of my people—
Alex, Art, all those who had stood beside me in this
struggle, who had come from the shadows of life to the
fulfillment that was Abilities.

Art and I began to hold a series of meetings with
the heads of departments, all old-time employees who
had been with us from the beginning. I recall one
meeting at which all we talked about was ourselves,
the management. I remember saying, "We have to
look at the whole story, not at just our merchandizing
or financing, but at the whole concept. We're a work
center of the disabled, yes. But are we right to have
management made up solely of the disabled? Have our
disabled people enough understanding of the function
of management?"

There was a stir in the group. It was a shocking
thing to say, I suppose, in a group where everyone
from the boss down is a severely disabled person, especially since from the start this very fact had been our
glory, our great claim to triumph.

"Why?" Art asked. "Aren't we smart enough to be
managers, because we're disabled? I never expected to
hear you say that, Hank."

"But I didn't say that," I objected. "What I say is
this: management is a special talent, a special genius.
The largest companies comb the world for real managerial talent. If you find it, it's like finding a home-run
hitter." Let me put it another way—could you run a
hospital with disabled doctors and nurses only, because you had sick people to treat?

"You mean, we should keep the disabled out of the
top spots, Hank?"

"No. What I mean is we should get the best management people possible for the top-level jobs, disabled or non-disabled."

This was a new and heretical idea to some of those present, but the conferences were designed for the discussion of new, even heretical, ideas, anything that might rescue this enterprise in which we all believed so deeply. I remember one night Art Nierenberg and I talked until long after midnight, both of us being ruthlessly frank. All that mattered was Abilities and how it might be saved.

At one point I said to him, "Art, we're going to have to evaluate everything and everybody in this operation. It may be that one of us will have to go. You or me or someone else. If that is how it has to be, that's the way it will be."

Art sat there before me on the other side of the desk. This was one of my closest friends and my longest associate in Abilities. We both knew I was right.

The problems we were facing didn't allow us any maneuvering space. That something drastic had to be done was not a matter of theory, but of practical necessity. We had lost a million dollars in gross sales, and there was the possibility we had washed out a research program that would have been invaluable as a part of our whole rehabilitation program. Our accounts payable were increasing, accounts receivable standing still or falling back, and we were having an increasingly difficult time in meeting our payroll. The short-term notes to the bank were past due. Further credit was questionable. Debenture and mortage payments had to be met. The solution—the only solution, lay in a drastic reorganization. To finance purchase of materials for new orders, financing was needed. This is common to all business. Art and I knew this perhaps better than anyone in Abilities. Each morning we would ask ourselves: "How much further can we stretch our credit? Others who have been waiting a hundred or a hundred and twenty days?" People were calling for their money, threatening to give us no more material. Our cash reserves were diminishing, our credit being stretched to the last notch.

All of this was a part of the picture. Gradually, out of the long meetings at which we were putting everything under the microscope of frank discussion and examination, the whole picture began to come into focus. We began to see the weaknesses and what must be done to counteract them.

"The board," someone would point out. "Let's bring them fully into the problem. It's a working board if we ask for help; a real working board that helped us to get to the top efficiency level, isn't it? . . . Or is it?"

There was no black-and-white answer to that question, or to most of the others. The board had its fine people, its well-intentioned people. It could be strengthened, it could help solve the crisis. These were successful, intelligent business men. They could play an important role now. If we give them the opportunity. We had not done so.

"It can't be all you, Hank, or all our executive committee. It has to be all of them, too. . . ."

There had to be more people on the board, more people who would get out and work—not just attend meetings, but help us to pay the bills. Partly it had been our fault. We had conditioned them to rely on us, instead of our relying on them. Now we needed them and new blood, as well as changes in our management concepts and in our board.

This was the kind of rough, hard, realistic approach we took. No holds barred, nobody's feelings spared.

Better management was needed, it was clear. The big questions of merchandizing and contracting with other companies, the special problems of Abilities—and the special abilities—all had to be taken into consideration and answers formulated. Every phase of our operation had to be examined and reshaped. In addition, all costs must be cut. Efficiency must be introduced at all levels.

We had begun one day in an empty garage and we had grown almost miraculously. In those days we were something new and everyone just cheered that we were succeeding, that we could exist at all.

Now we existed. We were for real. We had a great beautiful layout with all these wonderful activities going like a magnificent performance on a great open stage. The world looked on and marveled, but so many forgot that Abilities, the basis for all the rest (including the important research into the philosophy and people who make up Abilties), must be operated as an industrial complex, pure and simple. And it could continue to exist with only business-like efficiency, hard-nosed, able to deliver a quality product on time and at a fair price. It had to support itself, as a laboratory, in industry, for the disabled.

Let me say that none of these decisions was reached quickly. The meetings had begun, actually, months before my journey to Washington with the wrong film in my briefcase, and they continued long afterward.

On the management issue, for instance, we sought outside advice before we made our decision. A group of us, including Art, of course, discussed our problem with the top management people of one of the major aircraft companies with which we have worked closely for years. One of their vice-presidents told us bluntly: "In terms of management, you've been inbreeding. You won't take nondisabled, or, at any rate, you haven't taken them. But few of the disabled have a chance to get the excessive educational background or experience to contribute at the top management level today."

At length we made our decision: we needed management talent and we would take it where we found it, disabled or non-disabled.

There were some who objected to this decision. But I felt about it as I do about the teachers of the handicapped children in our school. When someone says to me, "Oh, that wonderful school, and all your teachers are handicapped too," my answer is: "No. We want the finest teachers we can get. We want to pay them the best salaries they can earn. We want them to be dedicated to their profession and to have the best academic education they can get. If they happen also to have a disability—some of the faculty and administration do—it is purely coincidental."

What we learned from that period of crisis was that the exact same truth applied to Abilities. With between four and five hundred workers to provide jobs for, we needed talent—talent in management, supervision, engineering, production, quality control, merchandizing, and sales.

This was an age of specialists. Nineteenth-century

Americans were not plagued by specialization. Every school child knows that Lincoln was in turn a farm hand, boatman, storekeeper, postmaster, surveyor, lawyer. Most Americans in those times were jacks of all trades, and masters of several.

Independence Hall was designed by a lawyer, the Capitol of the United States by a doctor, and the University of Virginia by an ex-President of the United States.

None were specialists, but today none could possibly have done any of those tasks. They would have to be specialists, degreed and recognized.

This was what we finally realized, and what all the top people at some of the greatest corporations in the world told us we would have to realize, if Abilities was to survive.

One of our greatest problems was financing. At the start we had borrowed on notes; later we had issued debentures for long-term financing, then we had raised money on mortgages. All of this meant that we owed hundreds of thousands of dollars, debts that had to be amortized and serviced. Beyond this, we had been required to procure short-term financing in order to obtain materials for individual jobs as new contracts came in. This too was part of the character of Abilities in its growing stages.

There were assorted possible answers to the financial problem, of course. We could use the modern technique of borrowing yourself out of trouble—borrow to service the present crop and to plow for the future. Some government aid was now available in backing for construction and equipment required by a contractor to fulfill his government work contract.

Moreover, both the building and the machinery belong to the government. Abilities, as a non-profit workshop for the disabled, was not qualified for this. It is a perfectly sound and accepted way of doing business. We simply weren't eligible, that was all. We could not even qualify for loans under the Small Business Administration.

We threshed all this out in constant meetings. There was some feeling that perhaps we should begin to think about complete refinancing. I knew this idea had many virtues, but I put it aside as a solution, at least temporarily. I think I was letting all of us sweat this one out in the hope of finding another solution, because I simply am not modern enough to be comfortable when I am in debt. And that's a weakness. Some of the finest companies in the world know exactly where they stand on borrowing and live on it. They and the bank are needed partners; this is an effective approach. Short-term borrowing I can accept, but I shy away from long-term. I still have a longing to be debt-free.

This was the turmoil within me. It was, in essence, the heart of our problem. Which way should we go? Should we expand, reach out, broaden our concepts of what we were and why we were and where we were going? Should we stay with the same simple work-out-a-way-to-do-it approach we had in the garage in Hempstead? Or should we take over the ever-wider-horizons approach of modern business concepts, using borrowing and expanding on borrowed money as a way of life, adopting the tool of refinancing as an exciting new concept in the kit of modern operation of a workshop for the disabled.

We had kept a fairly careful watch on our money situation; we always knew certain heavy expenditures were coming up, items such as vacation pay during the summer and payments on debentures at the end of the year. We had made certain fundamental decisions regarding personnel, bringing in new supervisors, adding new strength to the board. But I had kept the pressure on regarding fiscal policy. Hold the line, I had said in effect, don't let it get worse, don't let the debts pile up. If we can get some new work in, get some additional billing out, the situation is going to get better. We were trying to hold our position as the new techniques and management concepts began to take root, as new merchandising concepts were put in effect. Even as I watched this, I knew the difficulty; the sailor knows when he can't make the turn to home harbor in time. We were not going to be able to hold out long enough to make the turnabout we had spent so many anguished hours planning.

On the other hand, we had substantial equity in our property. We had built the plant, we had built the Human Resources Research Center, we had built the school, and we had put in many improvements on all of these structures. Although we were mortgaged (except for the Human Resources and the school building, which were unencumbered), we were in a substantially sound position with the bank. Amortized mortgage payments had always been met.

I personally wanted to see us completely debt-free, but in quiet hours the question came: Isn't your best course of action to go back and take the heat off Artie and the rest? To tell them, "Future forecasts for Abilities and the new program are so good, maybe we ought to refinance, get some extra money, some cash dollars to tide us over."

I knew the tremendous tension under which everyone was working. I knew that some of them, all of them who knew the tightness of the money situation, probably most of all Artie, were afraid to come and complain too frequently about the serious pressures. We didn't have enough work in the shop, we still had to buy materials for renewal orders on jobs we did have; above all, we had to maintain the operation, even though we had to let some of our people go. We'd been talking about diversification and we'd been talking about getting a product; we had made our forays into inventive ideas and our approaches to industry; now we were trying to buy time to hold our modified level until we could start going again.

We still had many contracts, but the big volume jobs, each requiring fifty or more workers, had been wiped out. This business for the big companies had been worth a million a year to us. We needed to replace it. Artie had been working on this problem day and night and things had been put into motion, but Artie, as he explains it, felt that he couldn't come into my office and glibly announce, "Everything's going to be great in six months, but right now I need to borrow $150,000 at the bank to tide us over." I'd told them all too many times that I'd never be happy until Abilities got rid of the mortgage, paid off the debentures, and didn't owe a cent.

So I knew they had held back from coming to me with every detail and I'd decided, "Let's work it out on a day-to-day basis. Let's do all we can, our utmost, not to go the other way, the way of borrowing. But if we have to, then we will."

We were sailing close-hauled, the winds too high and the storm too close. Unknown to the others, I had made the decision. And once I had made it, in my own mind I knew I was right. I had talked it out carefully with Uly Da Parma and the board. Uly agreed. I talked with Arthur Roth at the Franklin National Bank, while Joe Landow talked with their John Engle. We were reshaping Abilities in terms of policy and direction; we were in the midst of financial storms; we wanted sea room in which to maneuver.

And they said that considering our increased equity in the Abilities property and building and the general overall progress Abilities had made despite adverse business conditions on the Island, they would refinance the mortgage and provide the needed funds.

I had kept my decision and the follow-up to myself until I was sure the bank was going to buy it. When I came back and sat down with Artie and Joe Landow and Charley Finnegan and several of the others, it was like bringing the message from Garcia.

There was a moment's silence. Then Artie, sitting there in his wheelchair, broke into a wide wordless grin. I looked around at the others. I could see the delight, the relief, the excitement.

It was not a victory; it was reprieve.

The winds and storm still blew.

But we were, as Lucile had put it in a wholly different context, about to start out again.

## PART THREE:

# PLAN OF ACTION

# 11

## *Reshaping the Dream*

It was not merely a change in financing or a new man brought in for one job or another. It was, for us, for our lives and goals, a revolution, a growing up, a facing of reality.

It may be difficult for the reader to keep in mind as he reads this story that it is still, as it has been from the first, the story of a people apart. We are the disabled still. We are the mentally retarded as well, in recent years. We are the people who, until a few years ago, were largely rejected by industry. Abilities was the dream that would provide such people with self-respect, a true measure of independence, self-sufficiency, and a sense of achievement with homes and families.

All of this has been said and written so many times. But it must be restated here for one reason—what were we now, now that a whole new course had been set for Abilities? Where were we headed? And what part did the disabled and the retarded play in the new setup? Had we in some way become, once again,

second-class human beings? Demoted on behalf of the
great goals of business, production, schedules, products, profits?

I know these questions were asked by those who
were aware of all the conferences, the changes, the
new people. I also know the answers.

Far from a weakening of our interest in the disabled, there was a strengthening. We had brought in a
whole new area of disability that heretofore had not
been accepted in business—mental retardation—and
we had integrated these people into our programs—
industrial, banking, and data processing.

But more than that, we were learning how to use
the talents and skills of our people far better than we
had ever done before. It was our job to find the kind of
work each individual could do best. Part of the assignment of the new management people we brought in
was to coordinate our purpose and program.

Our people already were proving themselves in certain specialties, both in the banking operation and on
the line. In coil-winding, that is, winding copper wire
around a minute plastic part on high-speed machines
that revolved three thousand times a minute, our MR
and our disabled were especially productive. Their attitudes, their disabilities, and their satisfactions in
terms of what they could or could not do, made them
better adapted to this kind of production than were
many able-bodied workers who had a greater need of
action, movement, or distractions.

In evaluating our people, there were many aspects
which could be looked at from both sides of the job
coin. In one sense they had a disability, whatever it
might be. On the other hand, they had an ability in

their temperamental approach that could be a valued asset in business. Already the MR's had shown themselves to be equal to, or more accurate than, their perfectly normal predecessors in the limited banking operation we were performing.

We were now looking for special areas where we could perform the most efficient operation both for us and for the customer. At the start we had taken almost anything that came over the counter, whatever it might be. If it was legal and feasible at all and looked like it would give us a chance to keep our people working, we would say yes.

We were growing up. Still looking for a new product, we were no longer looking for *any* new product that *might* sell in the open market. We ourselves would determine if there were a market and, if so, what kind of market and whether or not we could reach it.

We had learned that because we were special people we did not need special approaches to sell a product we made. But we were still fighting prejudice. The man who goes into a company's office in a wheelchair and starts trying to hard-sell a product is fighting all the stares of that office and all the fears of a lot of nervous vice-presidents upstairs.

And hiring an outside sales force was not the complete answer either. The purchasers have to know whom the salesmen represent. The moment they hear it is a company of the disabled and the mentally retarded, a dark shadow descends on their corporate countenances.

"But it isn't that kind of a shop. It's . . ."

"I know. We have tried it, and it hasn't . . ." The

principles, have to realize that this exists; it's there and man pauses. He still bears the mark of prejudice and doesn't understand. We as a grown-up, mature organization, operating as best we can on sound business principles, have to realize that this exists; it's there and it will be there until we eradicate it by showing in each instance what we can do and what we can produce.

Our answer had to be found in new techniques of selling and marketing, new approaches developed by our people and worked out in cooperation with people in the field, either our own or outside salesmen. We had to have a product of our own, one that we could not only build but which could be merchandised, and sold at a profit—our own product, not subcontracting for others.

This conclusion was the start of the new overall program we embarked upon immediately after making our decision to refinance our long-range indebtedness. It was the beginning of a fully coordinated operation in which everybody and everything—management, personnel, concepts, products, contracts accepted, procedures and training methods, research and education divisions—all were to be part of a fully integrated program in which every individual had a fully evaluated working, yet still creative, role. We had to quit looking for work to keep busy and start looking for the right work which would pay a profit and was long-range.

What we had not been recognizing enough was that all the while we were struggling to keep alive, providing work for the disabled and bringing in the retarded, we were not only growing, but we were also gaining skills, experience, and understanding. Because of this, we could now function on this wholly different level without fear of losing what we had worked so hard to achieve.

Numerous countries abroad have set up their own Abilities. A company in one foreign country wrote to me shortly after our change-over. Could I give them advice on how to begin? What kind of management should they have? Should management be chosen from the disabled?

I recall answering them along the following lines: If you can find a really fine manager among the disabled, a man who can operate your company efficiently, don't be concerned about whether he is disabled or not, whether he has twelve heads or none at all. Take him.

I couldn't have meant this advice more. This was the kind of hard, tough principle we had brought to our new approach. I recall Art at a board meeting about this time explaining in his quiet way my attitude and his own:

"We have to keep remembering, gentlemen, that we are not like a business where profit is the prime motive, the sole motive in many cases. This is one of the reasons some businessmen do not understand Abilities. They find it impossible to walk that difficult line between their instinct for profit and our desire to fulfill our goal, and both within the competitive spirit. It has always been Abilities' belief, and now it has become its tradition, that we're going to help these people work efficiently and profitably, to be a showcase for the whole world. That we will do the Research and Training so that many disabled can be employed. That we can accept the businessman's responsibility and at the same time fulfill Abilities' responsibility is the 'almost' paradox—I say, almost—that many businessmen can not understand."

It was a very accurate description of the misunderstanding of many.

But Abilities, at last, had begun to understand itself.

## 12

## *Cash on Hand*

The most important factor during this period of self-examination and change was our willingness to face it all honestly. We had survived and grown; now we had reached a crisis and we took it in stride. Nothing could illustrate this more clearly than the continued warm relationship that was maintained between Artie and me during, and after, the night I told him that to save Abilities one or the other of us, perhaps both, might have to go. As I recall, I had said:

"You know, I'm not sure I'm in the right job, or you're in the right job, and that's part of what is going to come out of this fire, this bath we're going through. There'll have to be a decision as to whether we really are competent to run this show in the face of the crisis we're going through now. And tragic as it may be, Art, I'm going to have to make that decision for both of us. If I do not, then someone will make it for us. I would rather be the one who does."

This blunt statement was an indication of how rugged the whole reshaping of Abilities had to be from that point on, and Artie's acceptance of it testified to his complete devotion to the ends at which Abilities aimed.

Shortly after the meeting with Art at which I put all the cards on the table, I called him in and told him: "Uly DaParma wants you to have lunch with him. You better call him and set a date."

We had—by that spring of 1963—begun the reshaping of management, bringing in new board members and executives. Uly DaParma, former executive vice-president of Sperry's, later to become president of the Office Equipment Division of Sperry Rand Corp. was the new chairman of the Abilities board.

Art looked at me with a puzzled expression. I knew he was deeply concerned and probably wondering if this was his cue to start looking for another job, which he would have had no difficulty in finding because of his tremendous work skills and executive talents. He was, after all, vice-president and general manager of Abilities. But he just looked at me curiously and said, "Okay, I'll call him, Hank."

And wheeled out.

I decided to let it go that way. For one thing, I wasn't certain what Uly wanted to talk with Art about. It could have been exactly the opposite of what Art was thinking. Afterward, he came in and gave me a rundown on the luncheon and that seemed to me to sum up our relationship. I sat back and let him pour it out in that rather clipped, business-like way Art has.

"We went to lunch at McLoughlin's up the road," Art began. "I ordered a diet lunch, by the way. I didn't eat it. And I ordered a drink, because Uly insisted, and I didn't drink that either! But I told him about some of the areas that concerned us, me particularly, some of the paradoxes between operating in a cold, methodical, hatchet-like way that left out all the personal considerations for the people here, and the purpose for which we organized, which was just that—people. Yet, I said, we realized it was time we began operating like this if we were to stay alive, but we still had to keep in mind the basic reason for Abilities' existence. The people who work here."

Art sat there looking at me, thinking, summing up this meeting that was vital to him, and to me. "I told him some of the problems our training programs were causing, that we still need to train supervisors to run these programs for our unusual type of people at the very time when every dollar counts. I told him of the controls we have and are building, the kind of budget system I've set up, and how I am working with department heads and what I thought was wrong in many areas, and that you and I, Hank, have talked about all these things hundreds of times. I told him it was going to take a long time to correct a lot of these things, the little bugs that crop up in any operation."

I asked Artie then, "Tell me about Uly. What did he say to all this?"

For the first time, Artie seemed to relax. He sat back and grinned. "Well," he said, "for a while he didn't say anything. He listened. He let me get it all out. By the way, *he* ate his whole lunch. Very near the end, he said, 'Art, you have one of the most difficult managerial jobs in the United States today. That is no reason why it can't succeed. As board chairman I am concerned with the success of Abilities. We must not be influenced by large orders or large numbers of workers. We must succeed in the balance sheet of our original objectives.'

"And he wanted to be kept informed, he said, step

by step, as the reorganization and refinancing went on, every step of the way."

This was the kind of rugged self-appraisal that was going on and had been going on for months, and it continued and accelerated after the immediate cash situation was improved with the refinancing program.

By now, Uly and the board members, as well as management, had accepted the fact that what they were dealing with in Abilities was not its sameness to other businesses, but its differences. Any other firm would have had the insulation of running just a training program or an evaluation program, as part of their manufacturing responsibilities. There would be none of the research aspects with retarded and disabled persons. Or they would be running simply a rehabilitation program per se, with nothing else to worry about.

We had elected to take the whole bit in our teeth. We were going to build a product, several if possible, develop all the quality controls necessary not only to meet but to excel the competition, go out and sell our product with sound merchandizing methods and, while we were blazing into these new horizons, we would still do all the other things we had been doing for the disabled and the retarded. This was our program and we were going to follow it, even though, at the same time, our very life-blood was being threatened.

We completed the refinancing; we had the new mortgage and cash. The bank was paid. Creditors stopped calling incessantly. We began to earn discounts on accounts payable.

Meanwhile, other vital issues demanded my attention. I was working to obtain grants to keep the Human Resources Center training and research projects going, and I was trying to raise enough money to finish our school building without encumbering it. With one hand I was fending off irate neighbors, a few of whom did not want our children around at all, and with the other fighting for new contracts for Abilities. I was helping to recruit top teachers for our school's faculty. All of this was going on at once; all of it had to be kept separate. All of it had to be impartially evaluated and coordinated; Abilities' crisis had to be weighed against the needs of the Center and the school.

All of it was us.

This was how we began our new life.

The first great step after the reorganization of the financing was the reorganization of the relationship between Abilities, the Center, and the School. From the start, Abilities had been the heart of the structure around which the rest had been developed. The new structure put the Human Resources Center at the top. The Center now became the orbit around which the operation revolved. Through the research, we were able to learn the needs and apply the appropriate remedies in individual cases. We were able to train others and share all new knowledge with many in our country and throughout the world. This was the ultimate in rehabilitation, building minds and bodies, instilling concepts that gave hope to our people. Along with this, our education and work divisions ran side by side.

We were not merely shifting around bits of paper showing the chain of command, playing musical chairs. This was a fundamental reorganization made to solidify our financial structure, our understanding, and our method of operation.

To this end, we began a complete overhaul of our

fiscal controls. We had, since the inception of the crisis, begun a series of economies. Each morning we would go over our bills for expenses, trying to determine which ones could be eliminated, which ones reduced.

During this process, we began to see that we had, in our rapid growth, our eagerness and enthusiasm, actually gone far beyond our basic requirements. We needed sharper controls. We brought in Harry Levittan, an experienced comptroller, to help turn the corner on this phase of our problem and we brought in additional people at the management level to work with him. Also the people in our fiscal department needed better training. We found that we had been purchasing by techniques that one of our new people called "buying by the seat of your pants, without measuring in either direction." We had no proper controls to tell us whether we had bought wisely or too well. When you're a small outfit you can get away with such looseness. When you get to be the size we were, you can't.

In our reorganization we were trying to effect complete coordination of function and activity, not merely haphazardly shifting people from one bench to another or bringing in a few new faces for diversion. We were exercising selectivity; we were reorganizing step by step, procedure by procedure, in fiscal terms, in production terms, in terms of our people, in terms of sales.

Our new sales structure, for instance, was not developed swiftly or suddenly. It had been begun a long time back with our struggle to find the right markets, continuing markets. Not the stops and starts of expedient orders, but the solid long-range business which would keep our people busy for a year or longer. We were now a skilled force, we had the product that could serve industry best—including specialized skills.

For instance, there was our experience with International Business Machines, one of the companies from which we had tried very hard to get business. Eunice and Sargent Shriver eventually brought us together, but still nothing happened for awhile; the IBM people were very uncertain that the mentally retarded people could do the job we believed they could do.

Then Eunice arranged a luncheon meeting with Tom Watson. There were to be just the three of us, so we could talk openly and without any bright young men from either side screening our conversation.

I happened to get to the world headquarters of IBM about fifteen minutes early, and Watson's secretary ushered me right into his office. Watson is the outdoors type, does a lot of camping and skiing, a terrific human being, this man. His office was big, handsomely furnished, comfortable. His desk was clear of papers, except one tidy file.

We sat down and chatted about generalities for a minute or two, and then he said, "I have quite an interesting file on you here."

I said, "I find that encouraging. There's nothing I've ever done I wouldn't want in that file, Mr. Watson."

So we talked, just the two of us, and I tried to develop what I thought we could do for him. By the time Eunice arrived, he had agreed to carry out the first stages of a training program for MR's with a work project to be developed by IBM and put into our shop. Tom Watson had thought of it as good business.

This was in 1963, before we were at the peak of crisis but after we had begun to realize we must change our sales approaches and methods. I think historically IBM represented the first really different step into the new and untried that we took. It will always have a special meaning to me as a part of our story.

Over lunch Watson told Eunice Shriver and me, "You can count on IBM. We'll back this program for the evaluation and training. We'll get work into the shop."

I cite this instance to show that well before the crisis we had begun to coordinate our areas of action, though we still had a long way to go before we reached the full answer in total reorganization. You cannot reshape in a day or a month; the process is one of evolution and it comes about gradually. Faced with contract cutbacks, we had begun to find new outlets. Each of these played a part in our change-over, as we became more aware of the need to turn to these new directions.

The story of our first relations with MacDonald Aircraft in St. Louis has other overtones, due primarily to our own attitude about ourselves in relation to these great corporations of America.

Our connection with MacDonald also developed through Washington. Highly recommended, we were invited to come out to St. Louis and see their plant. Our recommendation had come via the Shrivers to Senator Stuart Symington, who, in turn, had told the people at MacDonald that we were a group of disabled people doing a good job and worthy of at least a hearing.

I had, in addition, talked with my friend Dr.

Howard Rusk about it. Dr. Rusk, besides being a great humanitarian and an authority on rehabilitation, is also from St. Louis and a good friend of the Senator's. Later, I learned that Rusk had sent a note of thanks to Symington, adding that he personally regarded our operation very highly.

I went out to the MacDonald plant for a conference with their top people, particularly Admiral Harrison, head of their purchasing. I flew out alone the night before the meeting and stayed at St. Mary's, a special school for the mentally retarded run by Monsignor Elmer H. Behrmann, a fellow member of the President's panel and dedicated to his work with the retarded. The Monsignor met me at the airport where we had a delightful dinner. Then he drove me out to the school, a dark structure against the night sky.

The priest and the sisters working with him were doing all they could for the retarded. With limited funds and facilities, they ran a good school, teaching the children to take care of their person, to wash, dress, and toilet themselves. They taught with love and devotion and filled the lives of these youngsters with brave new ideas which would mold their future years.

The building, the Monsignor told me, had been a reformatory, and then an orphanage, which was later abandoned. Years ago, Father Behrmann as a young priest had been sent here to reopen the building as a home and training center for the mentally retarded, one of the first to be established. The job he has been able to do, with the help of the dedicated sisters, is magnificent. He told me that he had taken this work on because of a dedication of his priestly vocation to these people.

After supper, as we sat in his study, we talked about my meeting scheduled at MacDonald for the next morning, which was to be directed chiefly to this question of the mentally retarded working on the assembly line. I told the Monsignor of the things we were doing, bringing MR youngsters into banking, clerical work, data processing, electronics assembly, and of future training programs we hoped to get into operation.

He listened very attentively. Finally, he said, "It's an age of miracles, this twentieth century, if you can do all this. We're having trouble just teaching them to brush their teeth. And you're making them into bank clerks and key-punch operators, all that." Then, after a pause, he looked at me sharply and added, "But I guess if anyone can do it, you and your people can."

It was a curious night. As we relaxed in his study before retiring he told me a story of how in the early days at the school he had been sent by the bishop to reopen St. Mary's, then abandoned and vacant for many years. For many months he was alone in the old buildings, preparing the remodeling and eventual opening of a school for the retarded. Frequently, as he went through the deserted buildings, he felt that eyes were watching him. And one night as he sat in his study he felt he was being watched; he had heard noises. "Then, suddenly," he said, "I looked up and saw the wildest looking man standing in the doorway of my room looking at me. I was a young priest and I was frightened. I asked him how he had come in and what he wanted and he said, 'I've been watching you.'

He kept repeating the phrase, 'I've been watching you.' "

The Monsignor told me he had asked the man to come in and sit down and the man confessed he had been watching him for weeks as night, moving in the darkness from window to window. "I realized that my sensation of being watched was not imagination. The man had been a mental patient and had been in an institution and then released. He was known in the neighborhood, where he lived, and was considered quite harmless in spite of his appearance."

It was getting late and the Monsignor led me down a darkened hall, past the Chapel and into a little study which, he explained, was the very room in which he had looked up to see the wild-looking man in the doorway.

It might have been because of that story that I did not rest well that night. But perhaps it was really only myself, my concerns. I remember asking myself all kinds of questions. Why was I doing all this? Why was I talking, trying to convince so many people? Was Abilities able to meet the broader challenges? Were we not still the same hat-in-hand operation, only on a larger scale?

During those sleepless hours I reviewed almost every aspect of our lives and activities. Did people really believe in us, in me, in what we were doing? Did the Monsignor really think we could make clerical workers and skilled industrial technicians out of these half-minds, or quarter-minds, these retarded? Were we only plunging deeper into areas that would increase rather than remove our debt?

I'm frank to admit that at that moment I was feeling

very sorry for myself. Here I am, I thought, going in to see this Admiral Harrison, on my knees completely, begging. For what? For whom? For the retarded? Okay. But we had fought for years for the disabled and we still hadn't even begun to break down the barriers of ignorance and prejudice. If our success were evaluated on an overall basis, had we in Abilities succeeded?

At that moment I was on the downbeat, but that is a part of this story too. We wanted to run Abilities in a business-like fashion, make and sell a product, then why should not I have such moments as every businessman and industrialist does? Often, however, with self-probing and -damning come deep insights. I thought of our disabled and what we had done to change their lives and broaden their horizons; perhaps we could do the same for the MR's.

Then I thought of all the doctors and experts on that Presidential Panel. Were they right, after all, to put the emphasis on the scientific task of seeking a cure, instead of a concurrent program to train the retarded to live fuller lives? Maybe concentrating on finding the pre-natal causes of retardation would be smarter and more expedient than training mentally retarded people to do real work.

I tossed and turned in the darkness of that small room, and I had a feeling once or twice that I too was being watched by that figure of whom the Monsignor had spoken. Only it wasn't his eyes that were looking at me . . . it was my own. It was a discouraging, depressing night and yet it had the effect of putting some of my anxieties into focus.

I dozed off eventually and in the morning I awoke

with a fire of excitement within me. Somehow, out of all that self-recrimination of the night before one great resolve had emerged: we would not go on our knees before the giants; we would talk to them as strong and independent producers who had something to sell which they needed.

After breakfast I thanked the Monsignor for his kindness and told the sisters I would return some day and lecture to their community if they would like to hear some of our stories. Later, I fulfilled that promise.

Admiral Harrison was a very pleasant man, and a very careful man who made it a point not to miss a word. He had his counsel with him and two or three of his top production people. We met in the conference room adjacent to his office.

The Admiral had everyone fully briefed. They began by telling me of all the fine things they had done for the disabled, how many had been hired, how much they had achieved for them in this field or that. I listened politely for about half an hour. Then, when I had a chance to break in, I asked the Admiral if I might speak with him alone.

I could see he was startled, I could almost say shocked. It was plain he would prefer to talk to me with his people present; after all, his boss had had a call about me from the Senator and it would be good to have everything in the open. Seeing his hesitation, I asked the lawyer if he would like to be a part of this inner conference, and on that basis the three of us retired to his office.

There I put my cards on the table. I said flatly that I

knew this was a suggestion from Washington, that it emanated from a senator, that it concerned a project that would involve their helping us so that we would engage mentally retarded workers.

"It's as simple as that," I said. "The experiment must be made in industry. Either we do it or we don't, either you want us or you don't. The President has asked for recommendations and action on this program. I can't do it without work in the shop. Admiral Harrison, I need that work."

I paused an instant, then went on, "Admiral, I care greatly about how many disabled you've hired, but I'm here on other business. You were called in on this retarded problem, just as I was, and it is certainly a humane project. Consider the alternatives. You can either take over such a project yourself and do it here, or you can provide the work for Abilities and we'll deliver the products to you at a fair price and on time, while we conduct the experiments with the retarded."

There was a further silence, during which I looked from the Admiral to the lawyer. Then I resumed quickly. "Could we face it squarely, for my sake. I've had a very poor night. I feel tired and a little disillusioned. I'll be happy to go back to New York and we'll forget the whole thing. You tell Washington what you want and I'll tell them what I want."

Still no one spoke. I wound up with, "But if you want a more efficient solution, put work in our hands and we'll hire these retarded people to do it. Your production and training people can help us with the techniques and methods, and we'll both have a nice clean report to make that will contribute to the welfare of the retarded in our country.

The Admiral looked at the counsel and the counsel looked at the Admiral. Then the question came out, the big key question: "Mr. Viscardi, how many people are we talking about?"

The answer was between thirty-five and fifty, as a beginning. But with the question, I knew the deal was made. Harrison and I have since become great friends. He has retired from MacDonald's but I still get letters from him. And he's never forgotten that conference, nor have I.

We went outside afterward and rejoined the others in the conference room. "Gentlemen," the Admiral said, "I think I understand this situation a lot more clearly than before. We're going to cooperate. Charley, you go with Mr. Viscardi; he's going to look over the work we're prepared to send to Abilities. Pick out the right projects and talk to me. Jim, what time is Mr. Viscardi seeing Mr. MacDonald?"

This was another kind of beginning. It was quite a time back, but it was the root of an approach that would later become crystallized in our concept of selectivity—we would take what we could do, stand firm on ground we knew we could hold.

There are times when we kneel and pray, even those of us who have no limbs.

But there are also times when we have to get up off our knees, even those who have no knees at all.

## 13

# *The Management Team*

Along with reshaping and strengthening our structure, we were seeking to coordinate the activities of management: the board of directors, the working managers, the heads of departments, the executive staff in the front office, and the special individuals we brought in or selected from our own people to head up training and evaluation programs.

Each of these key groups had its special role to play in what is, regardless of how we may try to minimize the face of it, a highly specialized production operation. The needs of our people, the disabled and MR's alike, are special. The problems that arise are special.

And the management team itself had to be special in its understanding of philosophy, methods, and danger lines.

The philosophy and policy of Abilities is difficult to completely understand. I get many calls from people asking us what we can do to rehabilitate a specific individual. Even though our story is known in the

main to many people, we still have requests to take in
this one or "do something" for that one, as though we
were a rehabilitation or treatment center instead of a
place where disabled are given an opportunity to work
and support themselves. A clergyman called to ask my
help with a man who had tragic problems. He had a
$75,000-a-year job, he drank too much, and he was
going blind. "What do you think you can do about this
fellow?" the clergyman asked.

We certainly were a place which helped people but
we weren't a hospital, an alcoholic rehabilitation center, or anything of the kind. I couldn't go into all the
details of our operation with him. I told him, "we
would like to help but we do not have any solutions in
this kind of case, or any place for this man. There are
other reasons for our existence, other things for which
we do have solutions, at least in part." I referred him
to several sources which could be helpful.

Those "other things" had to do with an efficiently
run Abilities which would support itself, if possible, on
its earnings. I am grateful for the job done over the
years by our board members, the effectiveness of their
help. The board, like the enterprise itself, grew. It reflected the concern and dedication of many people.
But it was, at the start, in many respects not a working
board in an active day-to-day sense. There is a difference between concern and dedication and rolling up
your sleeves and getting into the ruck and rumble. It
was perhaps my fault; I was the front-runner and I was
willing to run, and they let me. In those critical days I
believed the board needed the strengthing force of new
blood. There was also the fact that with the growth of
our research program and with the founding of

Human Resources School for disabled children, my time for the day-to-day problems of Abilities was limited.

Soon after our first economic crisis we began to bring new people to the board. We insisted that these people have an immediate concern with our program, an understanding of the operation, a willingness to think in terms not of other industries and how they functioned, but of how we functioned. We wanted no one on the board who was there simply because he wanted his name associated with a "worthy cause." We were not a list of names on a letterhead.

What I had come to realize was that we needed the active support of our board members in terms of know-how, creative concern, and constructive thinking. "What we need," I told Artie on one occasion, "is a hard-headed board that's going to come up with business solutions instead of you and me worrying alone about how we're going to borrow the money from the bank, and how to pay it back out of earnings."

Gradually, over the years, we acquired a board that was willing to take this hard-headed point of view.

E. U. DaParma came in from Sperry Gyroscope, along with Edward Brown. Joe Landow, who had been our financial advisor for years, also became a member of the board. Landow has been a voice of calm assessment in the midst of storm; he has a keen awareness of problems, but he never panics, nor will he surrender. I recall him one night at a board meeting, saying, in regard to our critical situation: "Something can be done, something has to be done, and if we look hard enough and work hard enough, something will be done. We should plan on building reserves now, while we're still struggling with the present, to begin to cut out the overhead that we don't need. . . ."

Landow was not just a board member sounding off; he was with us at almost all the morning and late afternoon sessions, going over the expenses, the overtime, the purchases, the phone bills. He discovered that our pattern of scheduling work had been producing increasing overtime pay that we couldn't afford. We were needlessly draining off thousands of dollars by this one weakness in controls.

He suggested that we put one man in charge of overtime authorizations. We gave the assignment to the general manager, Artie. The overtime cut back almost overnight. In one swift move he had plugged this hole of economic slippage. It was a dramatic example of the importance of effective controls.

We acquired other new board members in various ways. I had a telephone call from a businessman who had been interested for years in our activities, particularly in the Human Resources School. This man told me, "There's a fellow I know named Lou Raush who has a very prosperous company in Brooklyn. He runs it with his brother and he has time to devote to other causes. He's interested in your work and in the school you're building. Maybe he could help you."

I met Lou Raush and I discovered that he was looking for new fields of challenge. To him we were a godsend; he wanted to be a part of us, a part of our striving and doing, and he knew production and controls and effective merchandising, and I thought, "This is the kind of man we could use on our board."

Raush is a businessman with a real awareness of management problems; more than that, he understands the marketing problems of a small company. He knows the value of proper market-survey techniques, not for some great corporation where one set of tests will apply, but for a group of our size and structure, where the facilities within our organization play a big role. Raush didn't sit back; he took on the assignment and he took it on in earnest. He is frequently at the plant, examining what we do, the fifty or sixty varied jobs—soldering, incapsulating, riveting, making harnesses and wiring assemblies for aircraft, printed circuits and electronic components, observing the coil-winding and glass-engraving operations. With Raush it is a true labor of love.

In his recommendations to management and the board, Raush has a hard-headed merchandising approach. "You're not going to be able to sell directly to the consumer market. Certainly you can't compete in that market with this glassware. What you need is a finer, top-grade, gift glass product. And how do you dispose of it? By distributors and by working with and through other companies, big companies who can use it as gifts to their employees or their clients, or who have other special gift needs for which fine glassware may provide the answer."

We brought in other active board members, people concerned enough to devote endless hours not only attending board meetings but serving on special committees, exploring the best purchasing controls, the most advanced techniques of training and testing, and, by comparison with methods employed by other companies, the best techniques for us to use to maintain quality control in our electronic output. These board members participated directly in our total policy-making decisions.

Except for a few I have singled out for specific reasons in this story, I think the best picture of the board as it is now constituted can be seen not by naming each member and his qualifications, but by a cross-section picture of what these gifted individuals are like.

Here are a few vignettes, portrait sketches of some of these distinguished persons who gave so much of their effort to this corporation:

The president of a world-renowned company manufacturing office equipment has known Abilities from its first hour of birth. Aside from the tremendous demand on his time, running one of the largest organizations of this type, he contributes from his background guidance on the financial and long-range needs of Abilities, Inc. He has always been available for consultation involving managerial problems. Over the years he has had members of his staff spend substantial time with Abilities' management resolving problems affecting the continual managerial and organizational development.

An attorney and accountant, head of his own accounting firm recommended by our bankers in the initial days of Abilities to act as an advisor. This man, is responsible for many of the controls of fiscal-management approach to our operations. Over the years he has lent his outstanding background in relating our operations to Abilities' charter. He has spent many hours personally guiding Abilities' management.

An officer of a commercial company that does a major part of its business in supplying components to the automobile industry. He contributes broadly in the operational level. His extremely successful small company is an outstanding example of good management techniques. It is close to Abilities' size but has a different product concept. Nevertheless, the adaptation and modification of successfully employed management techniques to Abilities' needs is a major contribution.

An administrative officer of one of the largest defense plants in the United States has known Abilities for many years. He has an understanding of the type of work Abilities performs where a high percentage of our business is still defense work, and he has a heavy fiscal background which lends proper direction and perspective to Abilities' operations with its defense contracts.

The president of an extremely successful direct-mail servicing organization. He lives with an intimate understanding of the development of our bank and data-processing-services division. His company is very much the size of Abilities and his understanding of operational problems and the proper management perspective is a strong contribution towards our long-range-planning objectives.

Along with our board renovation came management and personnel evaluation. In this we were aided by outsiders from some of the large companies for which we work. The result was that we began to bring in new management personnel, men who knew their jobs from long experience and yet were capable of understanding and working with a special situation. We brought in as head of sales a man of real help in the field who also knew and understood Abilities.

With people of this type working with us, we were truly changing the country's concepts of the disabled and retarded at work. Too many workshops are too frequently uncertain of their role. They aren't business-like in any real sense; rather, they are something like day care-centers for the disabled or retarded whose families want a place for the individual to go and carry on some fabricated work that keeps him or her busy and out of trouble. They are needed, but this is not our role.

In prosperous times, of course, it isn't too hard for a great many of the disabled to get jobs. Indeed, in such times, our place is often raided for trained workers. But when bad times come back, work for the disabled closes down; plants that sought them out a year ago now have jobs for only those without disabilities, and not even enough for them. The disabled are too frequently the last to be hired and the first to be fired.

Somewhere between these two extremes there is a middle ground. We were close to finding it at Abilities, because with talented management and unique marketing processes we were seeking to find a real evaluation of ourselves—our role, our people, and our products, whether it was glass-engraving or electronics or harness and cable work. We, the unwanted, were beginning to develop a highly specialized kind of work that we could handle for the giant companies, work that did not put us directly into the consumer field, yet work that had a continuing, balanced, and, ultimately, diversified pattern—balanced production with defense work but also commercial products. Meanwhile, glass-engraving was the start of a product line of our own. This was the goal and direction which the new board and the new management team began to shape for Abilities.

Among the consultants brought in as part of our

research program was a firm in Holland. Its people range all over the world and speak dozens of languages. They do a very thorough job of studying a company's needs, and are experts in the evaluation and training of key personnel.

One such expert made a study of our coil-winding operation and he found a fault in the basic procedure so simple that we should have caught it on our own. The procedure was changed to make sure that there would always be enough inventory from one step of production to the next, so that if a worker on one step were absent, the whole operation wouldn't be held up because the workers on the next step had no inventory of material to draw on.

He found also that the loss of time and production was greater in cases where the MR's were shifted from one assignment to another than in cases of the physically disabled similarly shifted. The latter can adjust easily to change, psychologically, emotionally, and mentally, whereas the MR tends to become confused and thinks he is being penalized for not having done his work properly.

Our expert's report continued: One young MR lady was doing extremely well until shifted to another group. At once her production fell about twenty-five percent. It later returned somewhat as she got used to her new environment, but never to the extremely high figure she had obtained at first.

Informally, this management and training expert told me: "These people know what kind of disadvantage they have and at the same time they are very anxious to do a good job. Anxiety retards learning. The learning process is blocked when you are distressed, unrelaxed, anxious in any way. What we have to give these people, in my view, is assurance, continuous encouragement, and even more so when things go wrong." While more profound, it reminded me of Monsignor Behrmann and the Sisters of St. Marys. They believed in this philosophy.

His formal report to management urged a minimization of all changes and job shifting of MR's as one of the important means of increasing production.

Training areas were set up in the Human Resources building and the trainees were taught on machines and components exactly like those they would work on in Abilities. They stayed on these machines until they were able to perform at least seventy-five percent as well as average workers on similar jobs. Many of these MR's had never worked before in their lives; even so, under our expert training program they were swiftly brought up to this degree of performance.

Before he comes to us, each MR is carefully screened by the Department of Vocational Rehabilation. The DVR people have a full mental, psychological, and family background file on each MR, which is turned over to our people. Then we put them through a complete vocational battery, testing them in various skills—clerical, industrial, artistic, and any other area toward which they show an inclination, so that we have an idea of where they might best work out.

We use many methods to test their dexterity and steadiness, their overall coordination, their ability for clerical and industrial jobs. After all these work trials and tests are finished, we have a staff conference where we examine the scores in an attempt to get a general picture and make a training evaluation. Finally, we say, "Well, she did pretty well in filing, but not so good in industrial." Then we decide where this person might belong. How to raise the present programs of evaluation and testing in industry so that they will be suitable for these people is one of the research problems we are facing.

At the same time we brought outside people into management, we were making a concentrated effort to hunt down hidden and latent managerial talent among our own disabled workers.

In one instance we needed manufacturing engineers to learn what is called the "work factor" system of estimating the requirements and costs of manufacturing jobs. Instead of going out and hiring the non-disabled, we tested fourteen of our own people. Two of these tested high and were put into the training program for promotion to these positions; later, they went into the front office of manufacturing engineering and have done outstanding work. They are fully equipped by training to perform this work as well as anyone from the outside.

Other people have come up too, in a variety of ways, from our ranks. We regard this fact as important, because it means that at Abilities advancement, even to the top, is just as possible as it is anywhere else. The greater the need, the greater the challenge applies to all of us.

One of our original paraplegic employees, Frank Riger, has recently been made manager of the new contracts department, an executive post. Murray Nimser, who is flat on his back on a mobile litter, has been given top management responsibilities in the sales service department.

In promoting our people we try to achieve two things: what is best for Abilities and what is best for the individual. It is important that these two goals coincide. We have proven to ourselves that to stay in business and meet the needs of a changing era we must not let emotional considerations take precedence; at the same time we must hold, difficult as it may seem at times, to our fundamental reasons for existence. This has been the challenge to management. To meet it we, as anyone in business, have had to develop flexibility; to be able quickly to change directions, training techniques, and work programs; to bring in new methods of control as situations warranted. All of this we have found to be feasible, even in a group of disabled workers such as we are, provided you have the exact correct mixture.

The management team in action did, in fact, get results. As the new steps began to be put into effect, we sensed a change in public attitudes and appraisal. We were tougher ourselves, all of us. It was not a revolution, but a rejuvenation, because all we were establishing at Abilities was the result of effective action. We had grown to maturity; we were effectively competing with others and with each other; all the varied strands in our unusual design were being woven into a cohesive pattern of highly specialized, productive performance.

We were at last finding our unique place on the American industrial scene.

# 14

## *Diversification*

The man on the phone gave his name and explained to my secretary that he had to talk to me on an urgent matter. He wanted to give me a company. It had a valuable inventory of accounts, good will, and equipment. It could be worthwhile to us. I told her by all means to put him through.

It appeared that he was speaking for a service bureau that was involved in the great new world of data processing and had a valuable inventory of machinery and equipment of all kinds. The inventory of customers and good will they would give us free. We would have to pay for the inventory of equipment. It was a small service-bureau operation that had become overextended.

Board members Joe Landow and Bernie Fixler, along with a picked team from Abilities, went over to see the plant. Somehow, I'm always leery of things of value that somebody wants to give you, just like that. I didn't want to pick up any data-processing elephant to eat us out of existence. Landow and his team gave the place a real going-over. When they returned, they reported that while the gift and the purchase of the inventory were tempting, they presented problems and the possibility of heavy losses in both time and money. Conferences with our friends at Franklin National and two weeks of detailed study of the situation led them finally to the conclusion that this company was not for us. However, they felt that data processing itself and a service-bureau operation could be a new division at Abilities. We had already had some experience in this field and were eager to get deeper into it. But buying inventory and trying to pick up another company, even when it could be had for, in effect, a data-processed song, did not seem the way.

"A service bureau and data-processing division," Landow said, "would be a real step forward along the road to diversification. This is work we are not only trained to do, but are already doing on a small scale."

So another era for us began. We set up a data-processing division at Abilities. We had a trained and now expert corps of skilled operators in key-punch and related areas. These were made up of both disabled and mentally retarded workers, with a number of new contracts in the offing.

Our investigation of the company that the owners couldn't even give away had led us to a new area of endeavor which would use our special skills and bring in additional revenues. In addition, because of our friends at Franklin National Bank, we already had been indoctrinated into some of the basic requirements, by our banking operations.

This is the heart of true diversification. It is not merely starting up a few new "lines" that you can produce and possibly sell. It is not going out and buying up a few companies in a variety of fields, branching out in a dozen different directions at once. Ten thousand times you have to ask yourself: Do you have a special skill in this field? Is there something significant we can offer to this product or activity? Is there some facility connected with it—an avenue of distribution, a special know-how—that makes this an area in which we can fit in effectively and profitably? Is it related to what we do now so that exhausting controls can be imposed?

When we thought we had a product in the medical instrumentation Hans had invented, we did not pay enough attention to this principle. We were not medical-instrument producers. We were competing with the big boys in this field—and we were up against the whole hierarchy of medicine. We were truly innocents in the woods. Now we know we can develop this kind of product, but we know too that we have to look at it from a long-range view. The manufacture of medical instrumentation is within our scope. It is a worthwhile and important activity for the disabled and so it has a place in our production. But *not* as the quick turnover product that will save the economic day for Abilities, as we had once fondly and foolishly, I confess, believed. Now were we prepared for the merchandising and selling of these products. We began our service-bureau operation by using a small computer. As I write this, Artie and I have under consideration bringing in a new advanced computer for all our banking and data-processing operations. This, we believe, will upgrade these operations in both performance and speed. It will open up many new accounts we cannot now handle. It will preserve us from obsolescence in the data-processing field. We are constantly learning to use new machines and techniques in production, and finding new assignments and jobs in our diversification. These principles apply whether you are disabled or not.

Whereas Abilities had been started with subcontracts for war materials during the Korean police-action, we seek to diversify our workload and we look for our work also in other fields.

We had to put aside many of the old dreams. In their place we had some new and shiny computer-processed realities on which to build.

In addition to the data-processing division, with its general commercial jobs providing a steady and growing source of both jobs and revenue, there was our work for the Franklin National Bank. We still operated their Junior Banking Department, and recently we took over the preparation of their mortgage coupons and the processing and mailing out of monthly bank statements. The latter two activities are relatively new and are just beginning to reach a sufficient profit level to make them worth while. Both the disabled and the retarded work in these programs; no one regards these people as "different," they are simply people who work in Abilities. I often think that the terms we use to describe ourselves or others, however acceptable they may have become, are not ever as acceptable as such simple words as people or persons or simply human beings.

Almost all companies reach out to diversify sooner or later; for none of them is there a quick snap-judgment solution. Hundreds of firms have high-salaried officers constantly on the prowl for new companies to buy up. At Abilities, we had to build our diversification by developing skills, machinery, and training. We had to rely on our friends around us such as Franklin National Bank and the business leaders on our board.

We considered dozens of fields and items in addition to those we worked on in our own laboratories, such as the medical instrumentation. Most of these were rejected for any one of a number of reasons that crop up in business all the time: the market wasn't as good on close analysis as it had seemed at first; there was already too much competition in the field; the product would require more financing than was presently available.

Beyond these, what seemed often to be the key reason for rejection cropped up: was this new product so alien to our experience? Heretofore we had applied our talents to electronics, aircraft-wiring assemblies, and data processing, or related fields.

If the new product is not related to the existing manufacturing process, the best way for a company to diversify its activities into a different field is to locate the new operation elsewhere. If simultaneously you are engaged in the garment industry, the manufacture of electronics equipment and automobile repairs, and drilling oil wells, it is best to separate each activity in a different community—each must have its own management and budgets and controls. But they are all tied together at the top. There is one central fiscal corporate control and a meeting of the minds as to overall management and goals.

When we first brought in the banking operation, we were not quite sure how it would evolve. I was worried about Artie handling it because it might mean too much work for him, and might conflict with the industrial operation. Eventually, we decided to bring in a man to manage the whole banking operation, functioning as a division head and reporting to Artie. The banking operation was really our first successful diversification, and its division status in our company organization has been a prototype for other unfolding areas at Albertson. It was the first step in the establishment of the service bureau and data-processing operations. They are related and under one supervisor.

A successful diversified company coordinates its ideas of items it will make and market. One of our customers, for instance, has a furniture division. They manufacture and sell office furniture, items that complement other items they make, typewriters and office machines of all types. Each division is operated as a separate unit, but they all have a common direction, marketing concept, and selling approach. The salesman sells you all these ideas: the machine and the chair to sit on while using it.

Our entry into the glassware field, on the other hand, was diversification in a wholly new area. We did the research to develop new skills and a fine product, but finding a market was the stumbling ground. Ultimately, we developed, as a part of our whole reorganization and streamlining, a compromise plan: we bought the glassware, engraved it by our special process and sold it, often through a distributor, to large companies for use in their own specific ways, as gifts, premiums, or special promotion devices. Here we had a diversification of customers, firms in a variety of fields, buying different types and styles of the glassware we produced. Abilities had developed the basic process of engraving as a work outlet for the disabled and retarded.

We are now entering into many small related fields, handling many small items for a variety of companies, primarily in the data-processing and electronic-computing fields. It is better to work for many companies on smaller contracts than to work for a few on large contracts which may run out because an aircraft company is going out of business or moving to the other side of the country, or because a series of potential defense or government contracts is suddenly curtailed or cancelled.

We are now moving steadily into diversified industrial commercial manufacturing. We produce a volume of high-quality products in reasonable time with comparable production costs. Our staffs of skilled workers are among the best trained and most specialized available in these and related fields. They have to be, because when you are manufacturing small items in volume, say, a quarter of a million items a month, you can't afford many mistakes—otherwise you multiply your mistake that many times. This is why it is essential to have controls all down the line. Along with our controls, we have developed new methods and new training techniques, including the training of supervisors. The latter has been made possible by grants, and its continuation will, I believe, add a whole new dimension to our industrial training programs. This is an element frequently overlooked, especially in the placement of retarded and disabled persons. The supervisor must be trained to know what to expect, otherwise he will be unprepared at the outset to understand this new worker.

Already we have proved conclusively that the MR's, once they are fully trained, can match normal workers in the jobs they are doing. They like to work and they like routine; once settled in a routine, as training and other tests have shown, they can out-perform the average worker who can become bored because of the monotony of such assignments.

Profit is made in our kind of diversification in the use of the same or similar skills to produce different types of products in allied fields. This eliminates the need to train disabled workers all over again from a standing start. It eliminates other costs too: one does not have to buy all new machinery, erect new buildings, or develop wholly new sales techniques and personnel. This makes real diversification feasible and possible. You have to be able to turn out something a little better or a little cheaper than the other fellow. That is where you separate the black ink from the red.

We are, perhaps, only making a start toward the diversification we may ultimately find. I'm not sure. If we were organized for profits, if we were a great industrial combination, the technique would be to go out and buy up companies that look good, or look as if they have a real potential, pay for them either in cash or stock, and take them over, plant and personnel, all in one package.

We are not planning such an acquisition program. It is not our destiny now, nor is it possible. We are, and must remain, a work center where the primary workers are the disabled and retarded. Our people are still the basic product. Nothing can change this fact; without it we would lose our birthright. This is what we are—our limitation, our reason for being.

## 15

## *Marketplaces*

Etched in my mind is a glimpse of bitter humor from one of our early employees. Severely disabled, he had had an extremely hard time supporting his wife and two children until he had come to Abilities. Recalling some of his earlier difficulties, his rejection, his trying to sell magazines from door to door on crutches, all the assorted troubles and door-slammings, he told us this story. It was a satirical take-off on Jack and the Beanstalk and the cow he took to market to sell. "The trouble was," he said, "Jack had a three-legged cow, and nobody wanted a three-legged cow, even though she gave the finest milk in the land. That's why he traded her for a handful of beans."

Perhaps our man was going a bit too far, for ultimately Jack had the better of the bargain. But there is no question that the marketplace for the disabled presents its special problems. We have no right to expect it to be different; the industrial world is only coming to understand the true nature of abilities and disabilities. There are problems in our production procedures and our approaches and our fundamental philosophy that have to be faced squarely. One must help the workers of Abilities fulfill themselves, the individual to achieve his place in his world, one-legged or no-legged or whatever the disability.

Consider Alex, who worked in the packaging department in the early days and now is in electronics. Alex was born with no arms or legs; he has short stumps for arms and legs. He grew up in tough neighborhoods, fought his way to equality on the Brooklyn streets. Kids literally threw him in the ocean and he learned to swim back to shore. He sold newspapers in Brooklyn, where the underworld tried to get him to sell policy numbers as a lucrative sideline, but he told them, "No. I'll be a lost man if I get into that."

He tried to sell lighting fixtures, only no one would buy from him. Finally, he began to set days on which he would kill himself if he didn't get a job by that date. "By next Tuesday—or else," Alex would tell himself. But when next Tuesday came, there was always Wednesday. And hope. Pandora let out all of the troubles of the world when she opened the box, the only thing that didn't fly off was hope.

Finally, Alex heard about Abilities and came out to see me. We walked through the original garage where Abilities began. He pointed out how he could do this or that job. When Alex got back to his room that night he found a telegram waiting for him, telling him to report Monday morning for work.

Alex came in during those early days when our work policy was take-whatever-came-along. We were still in the stage where subcontracting on defense jobs was providing our only income, we were still learning production methods; marketing problems were in the future.

Alex today is a successful supervisor in Abilities. He has a wife and children and a lovely home. He drives his own car, bowls with the boys, and lives a full and happy life. That is part of the product, a fulfilled person accepted by the world. He still has no arms or legs.

The other side of the story is the marketplace, where the products of our people must find their way and their acceptance.

We have already told of some of our problems of marketing. The glass experience is an excellent example of what happened. We had thought, here is one answer to diversity: we'll make this product and sell it to the stores. Unfortunately, we did not succeed.

So, out of necessity and experience, came specialized techniques. Today we begin to know more about how to market-test; we know when to use our own people and when outside agencies are needed to get consumer reports. Making the product is only part of the picture. It must be profitably sold. In this little concept is the whole world of advertising, selling, marketing, inventory, merchandising—all of Pandora's box.

Most of our production reaches the public indirectly. There are, for example, the glasses we have been engraving by the thousands. They are truly fine glasses; one well-known artist I know has collected a dozen of them. At a dinner party one night at her home, I recognized them as being our glasses and, without mentioning that fact, complimented her on how extraordinarily lovely they were. Most of the other engraved-glassware items reach the customer through department store or gift-shop sales. We rarely see the customer.

While we seek to avoid the ups-and-downs of the defense product story, we are still working with aircraft companies, assembling harnesses and wiring installations, incapsulating individual component parts, making printed circuits and electronic parts. All of this is part of our basic production in areas where we have developed special skills and experience. We continued also with our original banking program and have branched out into new fields of data processing. In all of these activities, we are still one step removed from the consumer. Even so, we make sure our department managers understand the need of staying abreast of market requirements and changes.

Our banking service, for example, is performed for thousands of depositors our people never see. Yet the way in which the job is carried out is important. The fact that the work is always on time, that it has less errors than the work of many non-disabled and non-retarded doing the same job, are our keys to the marketplace. There were, at the start, a few ripples of surprise from some of the customers; when they saw the postmark, "Albertson," they guessed that Abilities might be processing their cancelled checks. One or two raised queries at the bank, but that was the end of it.

Remaining alert to the changing marketplace is a life or death factor even for us. A case in point is a company from which we got one of our first contracts. Before we could even get into operation, they went out of business, because they had not done research to keep up with the new plastic materials. They had been making their products for years and they expected the market to remain stable. But nothing, especially a consumer item, stands still. You have to fight inertia. The only thing worse than too little of the right kind of business is too much of the wrong kind.

In each field in which we operate we now have specialists to follow the trend of what is going on in other companies or other groups. In the area of bio-instrumentation, such as telemetering—a field which may be expanding even more today because of the space program and space potentials for the future—our people are working with medical agencies, with laboratories, with testing teams, with groups that can help us convince doctors and surgeons and therapists of the value of the instrumentation that we are developing. At the same time, Human Resources Center is able to obtain grants to carry out tests that will satisfy the medical profession, in part at least, regarding the practical uses of the new kind of instrumentation. We are constantly conducting research and demonstration programs to find new knowledge about the disabled and retarded worker, new techniques of special education for Human Resources School, new knowledge to make a better world for the disabled.

We do not deny or attempt to gloss over the fact that we have made mistakes. Joe Landow insists that without mistakes any company, or even a workshop for the disabled, would be dead. "We have to go on experimenting, reaching out, trying this, testing that, otherwise we can have no growth. The Ford Motor Company has the finest experts in the world and some of the most astute marketing minds, but they produced a car called the Edsel and lost five or ten million on it. A loss like that would have wrecked the average company."

But, as Joe also added, they turned around a few years later and came out with a complete new model called the Mustang that was a success almost from the first car the assembly lines turned out.

The fact was that the Ford Motor Company could stand the loss without a real threat to their progress. They took a calculated, weighed-and-measured risk—and lost. They took the next one—and won.

We have, in our way, done something of the same thing. We went into banking with the MR's and that was a calculated risk that we took on our own shoulders. Many thought it was a bad one to take, particularly at that time. But we knew we would survive, even if the banking program went under, and we were certain in our hearts that it wouldn't. Anyhow, Arthur Roth and his people at Franklin believed in us.

In this instance, I'm happy to say, we were right. What we did here was not only succeed in the banking operation, but we developed a new skill entirely, a new avenue to the marketplaces, to the world, an avenue of key-punch and tabulating and later modern data-processing and service-bureau operations. This is a whole new division to go side by side with our industrial operations.

The marketplace is really many places, after all. It may be a place where, as in Abilities, a human being finds himself or herself, his confidence or hers.

In the mock "marketplace" we set up as part of an MR training program, using a cash register as it might appear at the exit of a supermarket, we had our MR's calculating the cost of articles brought to them by "customers." In one instance, on one of her visits, the person playing the role of customer in this training game was Mrs. Shriver.

She came up with a large number of items and after they were all checked in and the slip added up, she picked up one article and said, "No, I don't want this, take it off my bill."

We who were watching were startled. How would this lovely girl Ruth, the MR operating the checkout machine, function in this crisis of the unexpected?

The patient training in the functions of this machine paid off. Now she carefully picked up the item returned, looked at the price, hit the proper keys that subtracted the amount from the bill, and rang up the new final figure.

It was only a test, yet for all of us looking on it was reality—the girl performing at the machine, the outside world in the form of Mrs. Shriver, insisting on performance under difficult conditions.

Ruth did it brilliantly. As she handed Mrs. Shriver the final tabulation, she was smiling at her victory. Mrs. Shriver was smiling too. She was obviously pleased and deeply moved.

# 16

## *Production and Producers*

||||||||||||||||||||||||||||||||||||||||||||||||||||||||||||||||||||||||||||||||||||||||||||||||||||||||||||||||||||||||||||||||||||||||||||

In the fall of 1966, I had a call from Mrs. Willard Wirtz. She had been visiting at the White House and had shown some of our glass engraving. Jane Wirtz is the wife of our Secretary of Labor. Since our original research in glass engraving was financed in part by a grant from the Department of Labor, she and the Secretary have always had a deep interest in it. She is a lovely lady with a warm human interest in the problems of the retarded and the disabled. She works constantly for the cause of the disabled and I am certain tells everyone about Abilities, our glass engraving, and the Human Resources School.

This charming lady had a question: Could we in our glass division engrave glasses with wild flowers on them? I told her we certainly could, any kind of flowers in the world. She said they didn't want any kind of flowers, only American wildflowers, which were Mrs. Johnson's favorites. The wife of the President was willing to consider the idea that our glassware, engraved with America's wildflowers, would be a wonderful gift for foreign dignitaries visiting the White House.

I told her, "We'll be honored and delighted. Has Mrs. Johnson any preference as to which wildflowers should be used?"

"Mrs. Johnson keeps a book of pictures of American wildflowers at her bedside," she answered. "I'll be in touch with you about it. I'll send you some suggestions and pictures."

We didn't wait for the material to arrive. Art and I put an artist to work on the designs at once, using local reference material. Shortly after, we had samples of finished glass with wildflowers from various states, including Texas and the southern states which naturally were among the First Lady's favorites. The engraving were on finger bowls and bud vases as well as glasses. We added an ash tray with wild stallions as a special gift for the President.

Mrs. Wirtz was kind enough to meet me in Washington and together we took the samples to a conference with Mrs. Johnson's secretary at the White House. Everything seemed to go well. We talked about production schedules. The samples would be submitted to the First Lady for approval. A few weeks after this, a phone call came from the White House. The President's staff had a new suggestion: Could we deliver ash trays for the President to give as gifts in the countries he would be visiting on his projected trip to Asia for the Philippine meeting on Viet Nam? These were to be engraved with the Great Seal of the President, along with a facsimile of his signature.

I said I was sure we could; we would do everything possible to meet the White House request. When did they need the ash trays and how many would be required?

The reply jolted me: "The ash trays will have to be finished and delivered to the White House in eight days at the outside. We will need five hundred."

I wanted desperately to fill that order, both for the President of the United States and his mission, as well as for Abilities and our mission. I wanted our workers to be engaged in a job of production for the high office and meaning of the President and his journey.

But I could not in honesty even offer to attempt it by the date set. I explained that the craftsmen who engraved this glassware were specially trained in doing this kind of work, that in the whole city or even the nation it would be hard to find enough skilled glass engravers to take on the job of doing five hundred engravings in a week. In addition, we would need the Great Seal of the President and the facsimile of his signature in order to do the art work prior to engraving.

"We can't do it in that time," I told her. "It can't be done. This is all hand-engraving, each piece is an individual product."

So we lost, in one sense, because we couldn't work it out. But we won in another, because later Mrs. Wirtz told me, "The President, I am sure, would understand. You only wanted the most perfect product to represent America. He wouldn't want it any other way either. Anyhow," she reminded me, "we haven't had a final decision on the wildflowers."

It all worked out quite well, for on one of the President's foreign trips, we were commissioned to engrave attractive paper weights as his official gift. In addition, Mrs. Tyler Abell, Secretary to Mrs. Johnson, advised us that the White House had approved our beautiful glass bowls to be used as wedding gifts, engraved with a decorative design, including the Great Seal of the President of the United States, and an inscription in the President's handwriting, which read, "With Best Wishes —Lady Bird and Lyndon B. Johnson."

Integrity is a part of the Presidency, the nation, or Abilities. It is so with us, I hope. It has been a goal that we have sought over the years, whether we speak of the production or the producers.

In Abilities today we have the beginning of a variety of production operations in progress. They are, we hope, carefully and effectively coordinated in a diversified way, whereby if we lose one customer or two, we do not rock the stability of Abilities in terms of income, workload, or working staff. Human Resources Center and Human Resources School seek income from gifts and grants to support their research and teaching programs, but Abilities must support itself out of earnings.

To achieve this, we have had to make compromises, not with principles, but with methods. We did not put in automatic machinery that would put ninety percent of our people out of work; on the other hand, we did not continue hand-operations solely as a way of putting ten people to work on a job that one man could do on a machine. We have to use some top production machinery because we have to be competitive in price, and we are. But total automation for our purposes has weaknesses; to us it is unacceptable, for in the long run it is not the kind of manufacturing operation we seek. In other words, we seek work that gives us a competitive position in a partially automated operation.

Nobody hands out production assignments on a

platter. They make you work for it, make you sell yourself, make you prove you can do the job. They come into your plant and check your management team, check whether you have the right facilities, the proper controls. They look to see that you have the best equipment and whether you have enough, and enough skilled workers who know what they are doing. In other words, they want to be assured that you have enough equipment for the kind of work you are turning out or seeking to turn out; that you, in fact, have the proper blend of industrial talent, machinery, training, and procedures that will enable you to supply what the customer is seeking. Whether you are a workshop for the disabled and retarded doesn't matter at this point. Their components must be manufactured to quality standards, delivered on time and at a fair price.

Contracts which come into Abilities today are evaluated—by our trained and expert estimating people. They consider the point of view of our specialties, our people, the potentials of this job in terms of our future, and whether or not we can provide exactly the right industrial mix to do this job best, fastest, and lowest in cost factors.

In our early days we were more interested in getting work into the shop than we were in the kind of image the job might create of Abilities. Not that we took on anything we didn't think was a good product, but we often took on what was perhaps too great a challenge to our facilities or capabilities at that time. Or we underestimated the hidden costs in change orders, shortages of materials, or work stoppages out of our control. Most of the time we worked out of these situations successfully, but there were occasions when we were late, the job was one we should not have taken on, and we could not deliver for reasons beyond our control. Sometimes, too, we made mistakes and our quality control was off. Sometimes we didn't have all the information and didn't know enough to ask the right questions, and sometimes we didn't have the engineering capacity for the job that wasn't quite ready for production, that needed production engineering. There were times when we just weren't smart enough to realize we had been trapped with a bad deal.

These are things we have learned. We have worked to develop, heighten, and refine our management skills and industrial capacity to a fine point of specialization. We are smarter now in knowing what we can do best. We take the jobs we can do best and deliver on time, so that the image we create is one of reliability. This has become a part of our strength. We know we have succeeded when we hear, not unthinking words of personal sympathy for our lot as disabled human beings, but instead, "Those wonderful Abilities people! They deliver on time and they're really competitive in prices and quality. Those disabled do a good job!"

That was the dream. Today it is almost a reality. We are hearing it more often now because it is what has been happening under our new setup and organization procedures. There is still room for improvement. We must be even more competitive than we are. I hope I will always feel this way.

Recently we went to an electronics firm in Kansas City with an introduction from a company in Andover, Massachusetts, with whom we have done business. After we had left, the man in Kansas City called our friend in Massachusetts to find out what he thought of us. The man in Andover told him that we had been manufacturing a product for him for four years, on time and at a good price. That was enough to bring us a new customer in Kansas City. That is what I mean by the image of Abilities, apart from what we are as individuals, how many legs or arms or hands we may or may not have.

In the marketplace we are not only a demonstration of the fact that the disabled and retarded can be employed. We are also showing that at Abilities, these same disabled and retarded can produce a top-flight product.

At the end of 1966, our work and production schedules included medical monitoring units, packaging services and data processing, service-bureau and banking services plus the production of engraved glass and the continued harness and cable work and production of components for electronic assemblies, continuing as an acknowledged supplier for the aircraft industry and diversifying by becoming a supplier for the communications and computer industries.

Among the great American corporations for which our people were producing materials of all types were the Litton Industries of California, American Machine and Foundry, Grumman Aircraft, Bendix Corporation, Gyrodyne Company, MacDonald Aircraft, Fairchild, International Business Machines, Ford Instrument, Western Electric, and many more.

We are proud of this record, this part we were playing in association with these great American corporations and their products. Yet I do feel that there are still further goals for which we must strive.

Even as I write this we are still searching for new products, searching above all for that one product or service that will be particularly ours. The definition of a product in this technical sense is one that is immediately identifiable with Abilities, is sold throughout the year with predictable sales that can be accurately forecast and against which you can plan manpower needs.

Despite the many wonderful components we turn out, this special individual item that will belong peculiarly to us, that will perhaps signify our highest production achievement in an individual specialized product, still eludes us. Our engraved glassware comes close. But we have not and will not give up this quest. The welcome mat will be out to anyone who comes to us with such a product possibility.

Abilities began with a reckless approach, perhaps because it needed such an approach; nothing else could have survived. We didn't take only certain disabilities, only one kind or another, we took a cross-section of everything, every disability in the community. We had the blind; we had people with artificial arms; we had people with paralyzed hands and legs; we had hemiplegias; we took people who were progressively losing more sight or the power to move hands or feet. And out of this mixture we made a production team. For all our mistakes, we turned out millions of dollars in goods of varied descriptions. And we did it by using a dedicated but reckless approach and the latent ability of these people and their drive to prove that ability. We put all of these plus marks together and we won. But that is all in the past, a story already written.

Now we were seeking new levels of production. And we eventually found them by coordinating our techniques of training and management with our new mentally retarded programming. By blending these new workers in with the disabled already on the team we found new outlets for our capacities. I believe we would have reached this crisis whether the retarded came in or not. The coincidence of their needs and our crisis highlighted the need for change and made it more urgent.

This was the real crux of the change in production. We sharpened up our methods, cost control, quality control, purchasing and cash controls, so that we didn't sit down at the telephone as soon as a new contract came in and begin ordering like a bride on her first shopping tour after the honeymoon. We bought with care and planning. If a contract was supposed to run a year, we didn't go out and buy a year's worth of supplies that afternoon. We conserved the money we had to lay out. We bought on a planned programmed basis and still at good prices.

Our people have to produce. If they don't, we cannot stay in business. I'm not saying we are better than all the rest of the workers in the world; I do say our people are as good and produce as well as anyone. And I will say this also: I think they are more conscientious than many other workers, because for most of our people, just to be working—to be a part of the productivity of our country, of life itself—is a great meaningful fact in which they take pride. There is among them a sense of purpose, dignity, and personal happiness not ordinarily found in the average working man. This does give us an edge over others, an intangible, but nonetheless true, plus.

In the case of our wonderful MR workers, the production pciture has some question marks because it is so often an individual matter. Our research is not complete, but we have reached tentative conclusions which apply to the MR's and not the others. The MR's have to be more carefully screened for the right job, more carefully trained, more understood. I think of one young MR girl who came in under trying circumstances, didn't seem to fit in, reacted poorly, and got into mild mischief when the supervisors turned their backs.

Her typing was poor and she worked at it erratically. Then some of our special training personnel worked with her, tested her further, took her off of typing and put her into an adding-machine operation. Here, she improved a hundred percent almost instantly. Perhaps it was just the change, but she was motivated, she was happy, she was productive. With additional training she became a very good worker.

Our training people in the MR program also tell me the efficiency levels of the MR's vary. This is true from day to day of all workers, but it is heavily accented with the MR's. An emotional upset may be the difficulty. Or it may be lack of retention. Perhaps the girl has not filed for a week or two; the training has slipped and it has to be recalled. That's when understanding comes into play. There is no rejection such as the individual may expect because of prior experiences. She is given to understand that her minor lapse in production techniques is normal, nothing really too serious.

She is sent back to training for a day perhaps, or half a day, and the pattern returns to normal. Usually, retention remains high if the drilling continues over a sufficiently long period and the supervisor is aware of the special problem. This is the area where we feel a program to train supervisors of mentally retarded and disabled is needed.

We have some in the MR program who "wash out" in the clerical area because of lack of patience or clerical ability, but who succeed admirably in some industrial function. This is true of all workers.

Could these people become high producers in the competitive world outside Abilities, these same retarded? The answer is yes for some, no for others. And this answer is conditioned by the jobs they would be expected to do, how well they would be trained and supervised, how they would be screened and selected, how repetitive the jobs would be. Each case is to some degree individual; so is each solution. We did have one example, however, when four of our MR's were shifted over on an experimental basis to the Franklin National Bank itself. They had been trained at Abilities, and they moved into a department at the bank where they were doing the same or related work, the only difference being that they were working side by side with non-retarded, non-disabled workers. It was a temporary work force which we had arranged to send into the Franklin National Bank as part of our research experiments.

When this was first brought up, and we picked the four (three girls and one man), they were interested and curious, perhaps also a little worried. "What will it be like over there?" was their basic question. "Will it be very different from here?"

"It will be very much like it is here," Mary Belowski, one of our training specialists, told them.

"You mean there will be people in wheelchairs?"

"No. No wheelchairs. But people."

They accepted it that way. And within a few weeks the bank was able to report that their record of production and their accuracy was as high as that of the other workers in the bank's office. This is an experiment we hope to continue, not only at Franklin but with other companies. It will be fully explored as part of our research demonstration program.

In the training division, Ellery Bean knows all aspects of its operation and has been a training director for the MR's. Few people have the patience he has, the know-how or the understanding. Ellery's approach is the realistic one: these are people who want to learn to work so they can be earners and providers and be a part of the production team.

His technique is to make it real to them. "They lose their interest at first," he reports. "But then, as their training broadens with real work, actual production, knowing they are going to get paid for it, their interest begins to mount. They do everything we tell them, they listen; as they work on the machines they try to remember every detail of safety and procedure they watched in the audio-visual training films developing their know-how for the big moment when they are actually on an assembly line.

Bob McVetty, Ellery's boss and our director of industrial relations, adds an important consideration: "Of course, before that, we tell them what Abilities stands for and take them on a tour of Abilities and Human Resources, show them the various operations we have and of which they will become a part at one time or another. They'll see the motor department, the coil-winding department, the harness and cable area, the business machines, the glass engraving, the school . . . everything. While they're still in training they begin to go on the machines, to work with our people. Later they'll begin to request that they get a spot in this department or that, they want to go back and work out on this machine or that."

They work because they want to work, Bob explains. The pay check is a symbol that they are producing. "But there are all kinds of symbols," he adds. "For example, when they first came out on the work floor, they didn't have badges like all the other workers. This was a big gripe. They had money, independence. But why no badges?

"So we had to steal a lot of badges, temporary badges that we had stowed away, and we wrote their names on the tags and they all had a badge. This made them happy. It made them a part of the team."

17

## Personnel and People

At Abilities we do not have personnel or personnel problems as such; we have people, we have workers. To us, they are neither disabled nor non-disabled, retarded or otherwise. Only human beings. No further classification is necessary.

Suffering—often physical suffering—is the portion of many who continue to struggle for the right to be considered the same as the rest of the world, not set apart, not considered different. There is nothing that can be substituted for this basic human right to be looked upon as others are, not honors, not pensions; no parades or subsidies can replace the desire of every person who has experienced disability to live and work in dignity, to function freely in the open world.

It is my view that all of us are just people, not designations based on disabilities of any kind. We are artists, musicians, writers, sailors, singers, dreamers, husbands, wives, parents, football players, radio broadcasters. We are what we can do.

When Abilities was first organized for the disabled,

people did not understand it, some denounced it, some said it would not work. It took years for us to change the public attitude, to get the community to see that the disabled are people. When we brought in the retarded, we had the same reaction from the public and also from some of our disabled. But when the latter saw how the retarded really were, they learned to accept them as a further step in our story.

But of course, there were special personnel problems in both areas. One must do more than merely find a particular job or working technique for the disabled employee. One must consider the questions of travel to and from the job and architectural barriers in the working area, steps and toilet facilities. To be with other workers on a job fulfills the needs of ego-satisfaction and self-realization to the individual, a need that exists in the hearts of most of us.

Those who think that Abilities is ready to hire any worker who knocks at our employment door merely because he or she is a disabled person is wrong. One of our personnel staff, who herself is a chair-ridden polio, explains that her first principle is *not* to hire cripples. "There is a big difference between cripples and the disabled," she says. "The cripple has something wrong that you can't deal with, because it is permanently ingrained in him. Cripples want to be treated as cripples; they want special service from the rest of the world. We don't have time for that."

In her talks to business groups, she likes to tell of one woman who telephoned to ask where would she spend the night; she had come all the way from the Mid-West to get a job at Abilities. Now, where did she stay? Where did we put people up?

She explained patiently to the young lady, who, incidentally, had not called or written for information, that we had no facilities for putting up anybody, that all our employees had to be able to get to work and get home by whatever means they or their families could provide. Out of sheer compassion, however, she told the girl to get in a cab and come on over.

The girl arrived on crutches—and wearing a mink coat. She complained about everything. We did get her a place to stay and because she had come so far, agreed to give her a trial working period. She lasted two weeks. She simply could not accept the philosophy that she was no more "special" than any other human being, and she returned to the mink-coated shadows out of which she had, at least, temporarily emerged.

On the other hand, we have brought in people with severe heart trouble and diabetes and the entire working force was always ready to help them if they were in need of physical aid. There is a tremendous compassion and comraderie on the floor of Abilities. But it is reserved chiefly for those who fit into this pattern of work, of production, of ability to use Abilities.

We knew when we began to bring in the MR's that we were adding to our personnel difficulties. These people, although in their late teens or older, were very much like children. They had to be treated as children and trained as children. And at first we had emotional problems and disorders, behavior problems and near disasters. They required patient training, and often did not come up quickly to the standard even after the audio-visual and other training techniques by which they were developed into full-scale workers on the line. Patience and understanding were needed, but it was worthwhile.

As I have said, we had expected a reaction from our disabled. To some extent that reaction materialized. There was anger, there was misunderstanding, there were mumblings, "Now we're to be confused with the half-brains," and the like. These things had to be dealt with. But they worked out.

We had also expected difficulties in the training of the MR's, and these also developed. The research and demonstration project provided us with a sound professional team and consultants to develop the MR program. To intensity the training program we brought in training and evaluation experts to assist us in developing appropriate procedures, particularly in regard to handling personnel problems. Ruth Kass and Chana Schachner, as I mentioned earlier, were among these experts. Ruth worked with us on a volunteer basis before she joined us as a full-time employee. Chana Schachner was a history teacher and expert in cultural education, who, hearing that we needed a training assistant, was fascinated by the challenge of working with the mentally retarded in a job-training procedure she herself would help to shape. We were, without question, moving onto new ground. "I tried to read up on the subject," Chana told us, "and found virtually nothing. There were few if any books on working schedules or techniques involving the retarded that I could find. The library people just looked blank when I asked about them. Except for the Research Team we had virtually no help at all."

Our success with these retarded workers has not been uniform. Each case is individual. One comes in and quickly learns to adjust to a work program. Soon she is turning out a thousand items a day, as compared to eight hundred turned out by the next highest producer. She is fulfilling a role in the world; she is happy; she doesn't even want to go home weekends. Another girl, with a pretty face and figure, suddenly finds herself in a world where there are many men. The girl is pleasant, innocent, and one day one of the men, a partially paralyzed worker, approaches her in the cloakroom. There is a scream and noise and much excitement in the plant. And there are those who cry, "Well, you see. It can't work out."

This is an isolated instance. It occurs wherever there are people together in any large groups. However, there are occasional romances in the plant. One MR girl, who had never had a date in her life, became attracted to a young male MR and kept asking him if he would like to come home with her and let her make fudge for him. (Many of the girls like to make candies and similar things at home.) One night the boy did go to the girl's house, and, under the chaperonage of the girl's mother, the two young people spent a pleasant evening together—making fudge. I understand there have been several other "dates" of a similar character since then.

Sometimes there are emotional problems. I saw one girl crying because a training director assigned her to a workbench with her face to the wall. She thought she was being punished! Sometimes there seems to be no reason for an outburst. One day a young male MR worker leaped up from his workbench in an apparent rage. "No, I can't do it," he cried. "I can't, I won't! The hell with it! I've had all I can take!" His shouts were loud enough to be heard above the throb and crackle of the machines.

But such scenes are the extremes and they happen

not only with the MR's but to some degree with all workers. Our industrial training supervisor is a part of the production team and with his realistic methods, is one of our most effective MR trainers. He begins gently enough, talking quietly and patiently as he explains the particular operation being taught on a simulated assembly line in the training section of the plant. "Then," he explains, "after we gain their confidence and we see that they are able to do some job fairly well, we begin to put pressure on them, just as a line foreman would do. When a foreman corrects a worker or complains at some error, the worker has got to be able to take it in stride. By the time the trainees get on the floor and at real work, they've been corrected enough to take it without their feathers being ruffled too much."

In the early days of the banking program, some of the MR's became upset because there was minor friction between our people and the non-disabled ladies from the original bank department who were later replaced by the disabled and retarded. "Some of the bank's original employees had been in the department for so many years, they naturally felt a little upset to see our disabled and retarded doing as good or better a job than they did," one of our supervisors wrote in a personal memo to me.

Virtually all of the original resentment encountered among our workers when the retarded people first came in has vanished. The disabled have come to understand that these are not just a bunch of "cuckoos" but people with a definite, if truly little understood, disability, that it is no more disgraceful to have a mental disability than a physical one, and that when these people can be trained to work as they do in Abilities, everyone gains.

One afternoon I walked through the shop with two industrialists from the West Coast, both highly intelligent leaders in the business community, both extremely interested in our whole program. They had not realized that we had brought in mentally retarded workers. "It was my understanding that you had only disabled people here, not mentally sick people."

I tried to explain that our MR's weren't mentally sick, but merely limited in their mental capabilities. "They can understand so much, they can be taught so much. Procedures must be broken down, work simplified, jobs methodized. Beyond a certain point, conceptual thinking is difficult for them. Just as you wouldn't expect a man with one leg to run a hundred-yard-dash, neither can you expect these workers to have high intellectual agility. But they can be trained to their maximum level, whatever that may be. We have no idea how high a level they can eventually reach. Nor do we know how much we can do with job methodization and work simplification in addition to new training techniques."

The industrialists looked a little dubious at that optimistic statement and we continued through the plant. They were tremendously interested and impressed and made no attempt to hide their reactions. They had never believed that disabled people could perform as our people do, particularly in our electronic-assembly operations. For some minutes they stood behind one girl, who happened to be one of our most efficient MR workers, watching her perform a series of complex winding actions, putting on bobbins to be wound, attaching the lead ends of the wires, operating the machine, removing the spools and checking them—all in a smooth, unruffled flow of movement.

As we turned away, one of the visitors leaned toward me and said, "Now, what is wrong with her? Has she a wooden leg or something? She seems to have no disability at all."

When I told him she was mentally retarded, he was absolutely shocked. "But she looks exactly like anyone else!" was his comment. I explained that for the job she was doing, since she was successful at it, she was the same as any other worker, retarded or not.

This type of situation happens over and over. A stranger walking through the plant cannot pick out the MR workers. They look, they act, they talk like anyone else. Marion Watson, who directs the banking operation so effectively, insists that her girls "yak" about clothes, cosmetics, boys, and dates as much as any girls in the bank. "They really don't go out on many dates—their families don't usually let them stray far from home after-hours—but they talk about it. Why not? Aren't they human too?"

Unlike the disabled, who keep the work program and their home life widely separate as a rule, the MR's blend their worlds. They don't regard work as labor: for them it is creativity, social life, it is reality, meaning, everything. This is why as productive workers in specific jobs they do so well. They actually perform as well as the disabled, and the average non-disabled, non-retarded worker as well.

John Morano is the production executive in overall charge of the industrial work program. His description of the MR's work capacity provides insight into the achievement level:

> These workers can be terrific because they love one area of work that others usually don't—work that is repetitive. Once you teach them the steps, once you know they have the dexterity, the know-how, you've got to keep them repeating the motions over and over until they absorb the pattern, until it becomes familiar, automatic.
>
> The amazing thing is that these individuals don't become bored. You see, they love it, this work, this sense of production. They just go on all day, and they practically keep the same pace from morning until night. Where the individual with a higher I.Q. would get bored and his or her efficiency level would normally drop, the MR worker keeps going and going on a steady keel. This is what is extraordinary and valuable to us, and to industry in general, once it learns to use them.
>
> Of course, this doesn't apply to every one of them, because the MR is just as much of an individual as anyone else. Some of them wander, they gaze, they want to walk around; you have to counsel them, work with them, get them into the work patterns, switch them around until you find the right spot for them. When you do, you find you get a spark, a reaction.
>
> They want recognition, too, of course, and they need it more than the normal worker, that little pat on the back. You've got to say hello. You've got to say it when you pass them—they want that touch of human relationship affirmed. And when you're

angry at something they do or don't do, you have to discipline them just as you might a child. You've got to make it known that you're upset, and that works wonders. You let them know that this is a job; you're getting paid for eight hours work and you're going to do that work, except for personal needs and regular breaks or lunch periods. And the kid catches on, this boy or girl, and the work is done. I'm not saying it works every time, the way we treat the MR's, but it works most of the time.

We lose a lot of our MR people to other companies, just as we lose disabled workers. On our part, we are proud to see our workers advance, but there are occasions when we regret it from the point of view of the worker himself, because we think he would learn more and do better at Abilities. One MR youth, who was doing very well in the industrial department at Abilities, had a chance to go with a supermarket near his home. His job there was merely stacking cans but he would be near his home and the money was good and he took it.

We were sorry to lose him, for his sake as much as or more than for ours.

Although the tangential personnel problems in Abilities are different from those in industry, the basic problem is essentially the same. Every worker needs to feel a sense of achievement; unless he can find a place where he can not only produce, but also grow and advance, he cannot be happy. And if he is not happy in the job, he, as well as the company and its production, suffers.

With the disabled and the retarded alike, one principle stands out: whatever the disability, the human being has no limitations that he cannot surmount if the will and purpose are sufficiently strong—and if we provide the proper education and training and the understanding supervision to insulate him with his unique job needs.

# 18

## *Achievements*

The achievements of Abilities, Inc., of Albertson, Long Island, New York, cannot be measured in terms of products sold, of billings, of gross income. It can be measured solely in terms of human beings, not merely human beings here but throughout the world. And if we are to measure accurately, we must take into consideration the changes that have come about in public attitudes and understanding—the lessening of prejudice against physical disability itself; the spread of understanding, leading to more operations like our own in other parts of America and of the world. It can be measured in the research and demonstration programs which have been conducted constantly on the workers and in the environment of Abilities, Inc.

There is a saying that imitation is the highest form of flattery. We want no flattery at Abilities for its own sake, but we would like to see the ideals and goals of Abilities imitated everywhere. We are proud that in some thirty-two countries throughout the world—in Europe, Asia, and South America—similar Abilities have been started. Many have been operating for some time and are highly successful. In our own country, hundreds of firms today employ the disabled and recognize their value. They are not merely trying to make a show of "doing something for these poor people." They have discovered a fine source of skilled workers who can be of real value to their company.

The story of Abilities is not just Albertson's story. We were from the beginning a pilot plant; the goal was to proliferate new concepts, new approaches, new attitudes, new avenues of potential achievement.

Part of our achievement has been in the realm of actual production. We have shown that the disabled and the retarded can play a significant role in industry and in business areas of all kind. We have shown that they do not crumble by the wayside, that their production records, their attendance records, their safety records can match those of any company, large or small.

We have not shown, nor have we tried to show, that these people of ours are equal in all respects to people physically normal. But we have begun, both here and abroad to spread the new doctrine of concentrating on the ability rather than the disability. We have begun to spread the doctrine that, outside of medical and rehabilitation circles, we should not even use the words handicapped, impaired, disabled, amputee, paraplegic, epileptic, cerebral-palsied, and so forth, in referring to any person. We have correct terms for such individuals, the only correct terms—man, woman, boy, girl, child. We have begun to spread the wholly new philosophy that all of us are in certain ways able and in other ways not as able as someone else. This man sings and another plays baseball; this one writes and another has an aptitude for being a physician, and so it goes. Disability is measured from the medical point of view, but whether the physician finds anything wrong with an individual or not, the truth is that the so-called disabled and the so-called physically fit are both handicapped. The physically fit individual is limited in his activities by his talents, his temperament, his height, his background, by a hundred factors. How many of us could drive trucks on long hauls, or even taxicabs in big cities? It has taken us a long time to discover that all human beings have multiple limitations, physically, emotionally, intellectually. All this is now becoming known and accepted in many parts of America and the world. This, too, is an achievement for which I think Abilities can take a fair share of credit. Where do you find a happy man? You find him at home, educating his children, building a boat or sailing it, growing exhibition roses out back. He won't be searching for happiness as if it were a television commercial, or striving for it in some institution as if it were a goal in itself. He finds his happiness in producing, achieving, and being accepted.

Over the years, we have served as a training center, not only for our own people, but also for outside corporations who want to see what we are doing. We have held literally hundreds of seminars and meetings for business and industrial leaders from all over the nation and, indeed, the world. We have had as trainees in our techniques outside specialists seeking to learn our procedures for dealing with our workers, the techniques we have developed for the workbench, at the machines, in the training areas. These specialists may be from foreign countries seeking to set up their own Abilities, or they may be workers in international aid groups about to be assigned to foreign countries for the purpose of establishing agencies for the disabled. It must be remembered that disabilities of all kinds are far greater in nations where rehabilitation is just beginning—Asia, Africa, South America—than in the United States.

Through these individuals and groups we have been able to spread the story of what Abilities has demonstrated and is demonstrating in its continuing dollars-and-cents operation.

As a result of the fact that two of my books were published in Japan, and that later a Japanese TV team came to Abilities and made a documentary of my life and work, I had become by 1966 a rather well-known figure in Japan. (For two weeks I was followed by two Japanese cameramen who took pictures of everything I did, even down to photographing me taking off my clothes and my limbs prior to swimming in our pool. When I got down to my shorts, I told them that was as far as Viscardi disrobed for Japan's television millions. They were very upset at this display of modesty on my part. "Nudity," one of them informed me, "is quite acceptable in Japan." I informed him that in Albertson, Long Island, it wasn't acceptable at all.)

Sometime later, as a result of my books and this film, which was widely shown in Japan, I received a visit from a well-known Hong Kong industrialist, Dhun Ruttonjee, a distinguished member of the Crown Council and the business community in Hong Kong. He was interested in the disabled. Extremely popular in Hong Kong, known to thousands because of his heroic activities during the Japanese occupation, Dhun called on me. It appears that a Dr. Harry Sy Fang, an orthopedic surgeon who knew Dr. Howard A. Rusk, had returned to Hong Kong and become chairman of the Hong Kong Society for Rehabilitation. Word of my work had reached Dhun and he had been filled in further by Dr. Fang and Jack Taylor who, as a board member and through his association with Dr. Rusk, knew all about our activities in Albertson. Jack had helped Dr. Rusk with the rehabilitation programs in Hong Kong and had been very active in the World Rehabilitation Fund and The American-Korean Foundation since its inception. He, too, had urged Ruttonjee to visit Abilities. The result was that Dhun arrived with all his geniality and his lovely Chinese wife to see Abilities and then to tell me I was needed in Asia. All he wanted was the answer to one question: "What will it take to get you to come to Hong Kong?"

I said I couldn't come to Hong Kong, that I had no plans to visit Asia at all. Distressed, he said he would like to send some of his people to Abilities for us to train. I said we would be happy to have them.

Then, a few months later, came a second visitor. This was Mr. Justin Dart, Jr. As I had been expecting to see a young executive, I was startled to find that he was a paraplegic in a wheelchair. Dart told me that the Japanese had discovered the meaning of Abilities and the possible meaning of disabilities. They had seen the disabled, sometimes legless, athletes perform at the Paralympics, which had been held in Japan following the regular Olympic games. They had read the Japanese translation of my books; they had seen the documentary film which had been shown many times on Japanese television.

He told me of a Japanese copy of Abilities called Sun Industries which was planning a new building, and needed advice.

"You're known in Japan. People have heard about you; they're excited about your work. We keep hearing about Viscardi. And this Abilities. Could you come to Japan?"

I told Mr. Dart a little about our concepts of freedom. "This isn't a government-run operation," I explained. "And that's part of the job that needs to be done—to make the individual feel free because he is able to work, to earn his own money, pay his own way."

I agreed that I would make the trip. It would include Hong Kong and Korea. Lucile would go with me and, since Jack was going in any event, he would travel with us and arrange the itinerary in Hong Kong and Korea, where he was well-known.

In Hong Kong I saw Dhun Ruttonjee again. Also in Hong Kong I visited the local office of Dr. Rusk's World Rehabilitation Fund, for which I was a consultant. Jack had been to Hong Kong several times before and had many friends there and in Korea. Through their local director, Halleck Rose, he had arranged for word of my visit to different groups interested in the disabled Chinese.

The result was that while Jack worked at the World Rehabilitation Fund business, I had a number of speeches to make, in addition to visiting hospitals and rehabilitation centers. Perhaps most stirring to me was to move among the tens of thousands of refugees from Communist China. In one block alone, one large compound, more than a hundred thousand refugees lived. They had huts, no running water, no sewage. Yet they were amazingly clean, almost immaculate.

I was impressed by the work done by the Maryknoll nuns there, particularly by a Sister Philip Marie who I learned came from New York City and New Jersey. I made an address at the Mother House of Maryknoll in Hong Kong to an audience of several hundred. It was interesting to me that my listeners included not only the sisters but also doctors, social workers, missionaries, educators, businessmen, and government leaders —a true cross-section of a community. I found the same kind of cross-section later when, at Dhun Ruttonjee's invitation, I talked to the American University Club and the faculty group at the university.

In Japan, in addition to meeting with the Japanese rehabilitation people and going on television several times, we went with young Dart to a place in southeast Japan, Beppu City, where I again met Dr. Nakamura, who had been to visit us, and we toured Sun Industries where they had set up a type of Abilities. It was in many ways at about the level of development we had reached in America when we started the shop for the disabled in the West Hempstead garage.

Justin Dart, Jr., who lived his life in a wheelchair, was deeply interested in Japan. He was also deeply interested in the fact that Japanese programs for the disabled as workers had not grown with the economy. He had seen quite clearly that more than general health needs and rehabilitation were needed. The Wheelchair Basketball Team, which he had organized, had toured Japan with a road show which aroused interest in the problem.

Dart had agreed to serve on the board of directors

of Sun Industries. They now needed advice if they were to grow as Abilities had. I was surprised and moved by what had been accomplished, by the new buildings for which the foundations had already been poured. Justin Dart, Jr. had been more than an inspiration to these people.

But now they must prepare to face the problems as we had done at Abilities. There was no way to avoid them. I told him and Sun Industries management I had only one basic suggestion: get people in the management and policy-making areas who know what they are doing, and keep them there. "If you have a doctor who knows rehabilitation, keep him in rehabilitation work. In the business area, in industry, get managers who know their fields." I told them some of our experiences in marketing and finding the right products, and I warned them that they should learn by our mistakes to run the business side of it with the best business minds and experience available . . . and they had to be people on the scene, here in Japan, people who understood the economy of Japan, and the needs, abilities, and limitations of the Japanese disabled.

I found that the Japanese were only beginning to understand the approaches to disability from an industrial point of view. This was not unusual. First we save a man's life. Then, as Dr. Rusk has said, we teach him how to live with what is left. In Beppu I spoke at a gathering arranged by the Junior Red Cross. Almost a thousand persons attended, attesting to their new interest in this field. Most were students. In Korea and Hong Kong as well, the best-attended lectures I gave were at colleges and universities. Frequently Jack Taylor introduced me and I showed slides of Abilities, of our people, the legless and the armless, at work; Alex driving to his job; the war-paralyzed working in our front office on mobile litters—extraordinary people who have made our company what it is.

I emphasized that individuals may be seriously disabled from the medical point of view, but they are not disabled industrially. They can work, they can be taught to work. And I emphasized also that we were not talking about some special breed of creature that we hide away. We were talking about human beings like themselves.

I went into so many rehabilitation centers in Japan where they turned out their wheelchair basketball teams, but when I asked if they had jobs in industry, the answer was "no." Developing basketball competition in wheelchairs is good as a sport; as a means of making the disabled individual a real productive worker on the line, a person who feels within himself the sense of productive fulfillment, the basketball bit appears to me to set up fuzzy values that befog the real issues. The same set of values apply with all company teams or extra-curricula activity. Many a star high-school athlete or football hero has gone into eclipse when he crossed the last goal line. I told them, "Your interest in the disabled is tremendous. But Japan is behind other nations in the development of jobs for the disabled."

Except for one company, I was unable to discover a single paraplegic in a wheelchair working in a factory. There was no transportation for them. They could drive a car, but they couldn't get licenses or hand controls or on and off those beautiful Japanese trains that go a hundred-and-sixty-miles an hour. And most of the houses are built in such a way that you couldn't enter or move from one room to another in a wheel-chair.

I saw some of the institutions and the meanings underneath. They were not new to me in Japan. I had seen them at home and around the world. I went into one room where they had a watch-repair class. Of course, I asked the wrong questions. I said, "Where do they get the watches?"

They said, "From the police department."

"Please explain that to me," I said. "Are they repairing them for the cops?"

"No. These are watches that have been found or stolen, but no one has claimed them."

"And what are the disabled here doing with these unclaimed watches?"

"Oh . . . fixing them."

I had to ask no more questions. The picture was too familiar out of my own youth, the "manufactured" jobs I saw, the endless institutional jobs that meant nothing. They would be fixing those watches for the next fifty years, but how many of these kids, when he finishes the course, will spring out of this institution? Some would, but hardly enough.

Many of them probably didn't want to leave. Those that did would have no place to go. There were no cars with hand controls, and getting a license was difficult, if not impossible. I found one disabled fellow who had a pair of hand controls hidden in a shed. He and I went out for a ride. It was a real obstacle course trying to work those hand controls, because you had to apply brake and gas with one hand and steer and shift with the other. Once or twice I thought we were going back into the building, right through the wall.

Jack Taylor and I went on later to a copy of Abilities they called Agape, a Greek word meaning love, in the sense of religious, Christian love. It was run by Takishi Ogawa, a young man we had trained for the Church World Service, a missionary and service organization run by the National Council of Churches in America. The National Council had sent him to America several years before to study with us at Abilities and build a Japanese copy. Ogawa and his wife were doing jobs similar to those we used to do, small jobs but real work nonetheless—packaging, assembling costume jewelry and record players and so forth.

I met with the staff and their workers. Jack and I were pleased to find a large "Welcome Hank" sign over the entrance of their compound as we drove down the dusty road after a long journey with some of the people and many stops at Rehabilitation Centers. We talked of their plans, their dreams, their problems, and the future. Later, at Sophia University, I lectured to the students and was given a citation for my work— our work—at Abilities.

I was honored to receive two other awards. One from Sogang College in Seoul and an honorary degree of Doctor of Literature from Sung Kyun Kwan University, the ancient Confucian University in Seoul, Korea.

The Korean disabled problems are much the same as those of the disabled in Japan: lack of transportation, architectural barriers, and few opportunities for employment. Lucile, Jack, and I were encouraged, however, to visit a paraplegic village in which a number of Korean War Veterans and their families lived. The village has a workshop with equipment provided by the American Korean Foundation, in which a variety of objects are made. A group of the wives of American military and civilian personnel stationed in Korea assisted the disabled veterans in selling their products.

We also visited the site of the Ruth Heyman Village which was then being constructed. The Village was constructed by the American Korean Foundation with a contribution by Mr. David M. Heyman, New York industrialist and philanthropist, in honor of his wife. This Village, when completed, was also to have a workshop in which the disabled veterans could be gainfully employed.

We also visited a fine rehabilitation center for amputees which is operated by Church World Service. The center, since its inception some years ago, has been under the direction of an American, Mr. John Steensma, a bilateral upper-extremity amputee who uses his hooks with the greatest proficiency. John had trained the Korean staff extremely well and was preparing at the time of our visit to turn the operations completely over to the Koreans while he returned to the United States to get his Master's Degree in Rehabilitation Counseling.

Because of the personal interests of Dr. and Mrs. Rusk, Jack Taylor and other members of the American Korean Foundation Board of Directors in health and rehabilitation, such activities have been given high priority by the Foundation since its inception in 1953.

I feel that part of the responsibility of Abilities is to reach out, as we did to the people of Japan, of Hong

Kong, of Korea, to the people of a hundred other places where there is need for care, concern, and a going operation that will help the disabled to find not only jobs, but self-respect, a measure of independence.

I feel that the disabled of Japan, Hong Kong, and Korea are at the beginning of a rennaissance. In some ways, they are where we were fifty years ago in America. I think that the interest of our citizens and their willingness to help establish independent operations like Abilities, and to seek guidance to do this effectively, is going to make a big difference in Asia, and in any other place where this kind of wholesome approach and backing is given. To me it gives a beautiful image for any people to express their love for those who have known disability. Perhaps my trip to the Orient, and my talks with so many of those who are taking hold of this problem in Asia, may also have opened up new avenues for them and for the future of their disabled.

# 19

## *Meanings*

The development of Human Resources Center, Abilities, and affiliated activities in the Foundation and the School form a record of not one man nor a few but of many who have worked to change the philosophy of the business and industrial world. What we were saying, in effect, was, do *not* be more compassionate, more concerned with what you call unfortunate human beings, or any other such meaningless approach. What we were saying, in fact, was, give us the opportunity to show what we can do in a strictly business and industrial area of modern life, and we will prove to you that we are as much a commercial asset as any other working human being.

To the extent that this change has been achieved, we have succeeded. The achievement above all else in the Abilities story has been the ability to stay in business, to survive the upheavals of business and industrial cycles, to grow, to expand, to bring in new people and new concepts, to have a business and industrial being of its own. And this we have done, not because of me or Artie or a few others alone, not the management alone, not any individual alone, but because all of us, many inside and many outside the actual operations at Albertson, have played their roles. In short, while Abilities, like any work center for the disabled, is a non-profit enterprise, subject to tax-exemption which it needs to fulfill its purpose, it should, as far as possible, support itself out of its earnings. Tailored to these standards it should endeavor always to operate under a profit-and-loss incentive.

It must develop a continuing process whereby more and better goods and services are produced and offered for sale. A great many factors are involved, but high on the list of essential ingredients are inventiveness, incentive, and investment of earnings in tools of production.

This competitive profit-and-loss spirit, difficult though it may be to achieve in a workshop for the disabled is the guardian of progress for the disabled American working man. It has lifted his living standards almost miraculously above those of other times and other places.

Without the sense of interrelationship levels of a business activity, however large or small, real progress cannot take place nor can real meanings be found. Human beings are not robots; the creative spirit that provides the answer to the question that no one has known how to ask is a part of the pattern of progress. This is the unlimited horizon available to all people, abled or disabled, who dare to dream, to question, and to react.

Sometimes individuals—well-meaning, I suppose they must be, in their hearts—have asked me how we

can love these people, see beauty in our disabled. A
child in our school, atrophied, twisted, warped, her
whole body misshapen, even her speech coming labo-
riously and with torture—yet to me she is beautiful.
Beauty, like achievement, is not a single thing, but a
cross-reaction of many things, of our thoughts, our
understanding, our approach, our needs, our philosophy.

Some of the world's most beautiful people could
have known physical disability. Homer could have
squatted in the dust at the gates of Athens and the rich
Athenians might have pitied him as they passed and
tossed a drachma or two in his cap. He was totally
sightless, yet his poetry is read and loved today, thousands of years later. Milton was blind, too, and so was
Prescott the historian. Julius Caesar was an epileptic,
as was Van Gogh, who painted the sunlight and the
stars. Where is beauty? It is more than in the eyes of
the beholder; it is in the heart of the beholder, in his
understanding.

Part of our responsibility also is to demonstrate that
adversity does not have to be total disaster. Our people
have known suffering, but I do not suggest that only
by the kind of adversity they have known can character be formed. Many of the great men and women of
the world who had no disabilities had to fight through
adversity, grief, afflictions; many of the greatest are
molded in the crucible of suffering. Often such experiences serve to shape and stir the depths of potentials.
The crippled child strains her fingers and draws the
brightly colored flower against the bright crayon blue
sky.

Part of our meaning is that we must dare to upset

some of the old ideas, especially in the world of the disabled. One of the reasons for our success is that we haven't gone for that ancient cliché about putting square pegs in square holes and round pegs in round holes.

This is to me one of the most tattered and over-worked principles in business or industry. In the first place, it implies that all pegs—and presumably all people—are neatly and conveniently pre-shaped and all we need to do is determine the shape and flip the peg into the proper hole. Presto! The peg is adjusted and comfortable and management can rest assured that the maximum efficient use is being made of it. But this overlooks one important point. Putting the square peg in the square hole is the surest way of denying it room for improvement or expansion. We have to have room to grow, people have to have reason to grow. Life cannot be made to fit into the images the efficiency experts evolve. It is the exceptional men and women who advance civilization, who create and build the cities of the great. Our disabled people are among them.

We have shown at Abilities that wherever there is a challenge there is an answer, some kind of answer. Few men suspect the full measure of their capabilities until put to the test; many resist change, resist trying a new job, a new way, a new idea. We learn only as we dare to meet the challenge of the new with a blend of judgement, maturity, and courage. This is true at all levels, from the newest worker on the bench to the chairman of the board. Putting square pegs in square holes may get an organization started, but the story cannot stop there. Human beings, disabled or not, are many-sided and just about the time we think we have them correctly pegged, another side shows up. Perhaps square pegs in round holes can stir up incentive in a way we have not understood. In any case, one purpose of our operations at Abilities is to show that square peg-legs are not necessarily limited to the square hole of the sheltered workshop and "made-work" programs of the past, nor should they be denied because they do not fit neatly into the perfect image of the recruitment and industrial medical evaluation.

One of our workers, Peter, about whom I wrote in an earlier book, *A Laughter In The Lonely Night,* was a tall youth who suffered from dystonia, a rare ailment which made it impossible for him to walk properly or stand. Yet we worked out ways for this boy to work. Later, he had an operation on the brain which restored to him eighty percent of normal action. He was always impatient with assignments inside the factory, he wanted to work outdoors. We let him drive a truck; he got a chauffeur's license and became a pretty good driver. Then he came to me with a secret ambition! He wanted to go to sea, to join the Merchant Marine. Ultimately, Peter was accepted by the Grace Lines and shipped out on a liner bound for distant ports. I had a letter from him telling me of his experiences and achievements; that although he still had some difficulty in walking, he was able to ride the sea on this ship, never once fell or slipped because of the roll or pitch in storms.

Peter's job on board was that of a general utility seaman; they used him wherever the need was. But in his letter, he told me of his plans and hopes: "I looked over the whole ship and I would like to work in the engine department. This department is the only one in which I can learn a trade that I can use ashore. I would start as a wiper. After six months, you can take a Coast Guard test for a fireman. His job is a stationary one, watching, regulating, and cleaning the burners. And, Hank, I don't have to stop there. I can take my tests and with experience get to be an engineer. . . ."

Always in my dealings with our disabled people I have emphasized that they must look not for security, for it doesn't exist for them any more than it exists for any man. If our forefathers had not had the courage to take a chance, there never would have been an America as we know it.

All people and things are engaged in the making of history. The legacy we leave to the future is what we do in the present. The glacier leaves its striations on the rock, the winds sculpt the sands and stones, ideas and hands and voices leave their imprint on the minds and manners of mankind.

I cannot be sure what we at Abilities will leave. We will at least have changed a few lives, have broken down a few prejudices. I would hope especially that we have broken down the prejudices in the world of industry regarding the disabled and the retarded workers. As time goes on, the working force of the disabled should be of increasing importance to American industry, to the industry of the world, at all levels and in all areas. It is by recognizing their role and their potential that business and industry can best play their part in relation to these people.

Perhaps, in another generation, a mother holding a crippled child to her breast with the prayer that he may live a full rich life, with dignity and self-sufficiency, may have the comfort of knowing that this prayer is within the realm of realistic fulfillment because of what Abilities as a pilot plant, with the co-operation of American business and industry, has done to lead the way.

## 20

## *Futures*

At a luncheon recently, the president of a large American corporation asked me if I did not think that Abilities had made its point to the world, had reached its goal. My answer was, "We have only begun. There are still millions of the disabled and retarded, perhaps as many as ten millions in America this moment, who do not have regular employment and cannot find it. We have pointed out a road. We have not reached our destination."

Where will we go? The answer lies in understanding and integrity—yours, mine, the people at Abilities, the people in the industrial world—integrity to ourselves and to our communities. With understanding and integrity, in our production, skills, workmanship, and meaning, we can continue to lead the way. In this respect, I like to think that we at Abilities, both as a work center and as individuals, represent something important in the American community. I liken ourselves and what we do as a mirror to the world, all of us at Abilities, management, training staff, supervisors, foremen, and workers. A good mirror reflects a true likeness and image; the mirror with a flaw gives a distorted and untrue image; the shattered mirror gives a shattered image that can be almost unrecognizable. The image we want the world to see is what we are as people, what we can be as producers. When we deliver the product of integrity—our skilled workmanship and high quality standards on schedule—we are giving the image of our real selves.

We began with the determination that we could change the world in which we live, first for ourselves and then for others like us. In some small measure we have succeeded, but it is still our purpose to fulfill our goals for generations of disabled people not yet born.

It is my conviction that few who come to the Human Resources Center, or the Human Resources School with its extraordinary children, or to Abilities itself, can ever forget their visit. Long after the dates or names of any or all of us may be forgotten, the picture of the stirring drive of these people remains, with all its excitement and depth of meaning.

This is our part of Abilities' mission, as a self-supporting work center, for today, tomorrow, and the days to come—to reflect the image of who and what we really are, and thereby influence and change the lives of millions of human beings in this world.

# INDEX

*INDEX*